UNITED STATES DISTRICT COURT
SOUTHERN DISTRICT OF NEW YORK
------------------------------------------------------------X
WARNER BROS. ENTERTAINMENT INC. and
J.K. ROWLING,

                           Plaintiffs,

                  - against -

RDR BOOKS and DOES 1-10,

                         Defendants.
------------------------------------------------------------X

07 Civ. 9667 (RPP)

**OPINION & ORDER**

**ROBERT P. PATTERSON, JR., U.S.D.J.**

On October 31, 2007, Plaintiffs Warner Bros. Entertainment Inc. and J.K. Rowling commenced this action against Defendant RDR Books, alleging copyright infringement pursuant to 17 U.S.C. §§ 101 *et seq.*, as well as several other federal and state claims, and seeking both injunctive relief and damages. By order dated March 5, 2008, the Court consolidated the scheduled evidentiary hearing on Plaintiffs' motion for a preliminary injunction[1] with a trial on the merits pursuant to Federal Rule of Civil Procedure 65(a)(2). By their pretrial orders, the parties narrowed the claims and defenses to be tried: Plaintiffs pursued only their claims for copyright infringement and statutory damages under 17 U.S.C. §§ 101 *et seq.* of the Copyright Act; Defendant pursued only its defenses and affirmative defenses of copyright fair use under 17 U.S.C. § 107, copyright misuse, and unclean hands. The Court held a bench trial on the merits from April 14,

---

[1] Prior to the Court's present ruling, Defendant was under a temporary restraining order issued by the Court, with consent of the parties' attorneys, on November 8, 2007. Pursuant to that order, Defendant was temporarily restrained from completing the typesetting of the allegedly infringing book, from printing the book and distributing the same to the public for sale, and from advertising, promoting, soliciting, licensing, or accepting orders for the book in the United States of America and abroad. Doc. 92

2008 to April 17, 2008. This opinion constitutes the Court's findings of fact and conclusions of law pursuant to Federal Rule of Civil Procedure 52(a).

**FINDINGS OF FACT**

**I.     The Copyrighted Works**

Plaintiff J.K. Rowling ("Rowling") is the author of the highly acclaimed Harry Potter book series. (Tr. (Rowling) at 43:6-7, 47:17-20; Pl. Ex. 25 (Rowling Decl.) at ¶1.) Written for children but enjoyed by children and adults alike, the Harry Potter series chronicles the lives and adventures of Harry Potter and his friends as they come of age at the Hogwarts School of Witchcraft and Wizardry and face the evil Lord Voldemort. (Pl. Ex. 25 (Rowling Decl.) at ¶ 2.) It is a tale of a fictional world filled with magical spells, fantastical creatures, and imaginary places and things. (Tr. (Vander Ark) at 346:1-6; 371:1-22; id. (Sorensen) at 513:6-14.)

Rowling published the first of seven books in the series, Harry Potter and the Philosopher's Stone, in the United Kingdom in 1997. (Tr. (Rowling) at 46:12-16; id. (Vander Ark) at 363:19-20.) In 1998, the first book was published in the United States as Harry Potter and the Sorcerer's Stone. (Pl. Ex. 25 (Rowling Decl.) at ¶ 2.) Over the next ten years, Rowling wrote and published the remaining six books in the Harry Potter series (Id.): Harry Potter and the Chamber of Secrets (1998), Harry Potter and the Prisoner of Azkaban (1999), Harry Potter and the Goblet of Fire (2000), Harry Potter and the Order of the Phoenix (2003), and Harry Potter and the Half-Blood Prince (2005). (Pl. Exs. 5-9.) The seventh and final book, Harry Potter and the Deathly Hallows was released on July 21, 2007. (Pl. Ex. 10). Rowling owns a United States copyright in each of the Harry Potter books. (Pl. Ex. 12 (Blair Decl.) at ¶ 4; Pl. Ex. 12A; Tr. (Rowling) at 43:8-9.)

The Harry Potter series has achieved enormous popularity and phenomenal sales. (Tr. (Murphy) at 432:20-433:3; id. (Harris) at 443:16-18). The books have won numerous awards, including children's literary awards and the British Book Award. (Id. (Rowling) at 47:17-20). Most gratifying to Rowling is that the Harry Potter series has been credited with encouraging readership among children. (Id. (Rowling) at 103:8-22.)

As a result of the success of the Harry Potter books, Plaintiff Warner Bros. Entertainment Inc. ("Warner Brothers") obtained from Rowling the exclusive film rights to the entire seven-book Harry Potter series. (Pl. Ex. 26 (Williams Decl.) at ¶ 3.) Warner Brothers is the exclusive distributor for worldwide distribution of these films. (Id. at ¶ 4.) To date, Warner Brothers has released five Harry Potter films, and the sixth is scheduled for a worldwide release in November 2008. (Id. at ¶¶ 3, 4.) Each of the Harry Potter films is the subject of a copyright registration. (Id. at ¶ 3.) Warner Brothers licensed certain rights to Electronic Arts to create video games based on the Harry Potter books and films, which included a series of "Famous Wizard Cards" that Rowling created and which are the subject of U.S. copyright registrations jointly owned by Warner Brothers and Electronic Arts. (Tr. (Rowling) at 76:15-17; Pl. Post-trial Br., Ex. B.)

Early on in the publication of the Harry Potter series, Rowling wrote a short series of fictional newspapers entitled "The Daily Prophet," which were published and distributed to fans in the United Kingdom. (Tr. (Rowling) at 73:17 74:1.) Rowling owns a U.K. copyright in "The Daily Prophet" newsletters. (Tr. (Rowling) at 74:6-7; see Pl. Post-trial Br., Ex. A.)

In addition, Rowling wrote two short companion books to the Harry Potter series (the "companion books"), the royalties from which she donated to the charity Comic

Relief. (Tr. (Rowling) at 49:12-50:10.) The first, Quidditch Through the Ages (2001), recounts the history and development of "quidditch," an imaginary sport featured in the Harry Potter series that involves teams of witches and wizards on flying broomsticks. (Pl. Ex. 2.) The second, Fantastic Beasts & Where to Find Them (2001), is an A-to-Z encyclopedia of the imaginary beasts and beings that exist in Harry Potter's fictional world. (Pl. Ex. 3.) Both appear in the Harry Potter series as textbooks that the students at Hogwarts use in their studies, and the companion books are marketed as such. Neither of the companion books is written in narrative form; instead each book chronicles and expands on the fictional facts that unfold in the Harry Potter series. (Tr. (Vander Ark) at 396:21-25; see Pl. Exs. 2-3.) The companion books are both registered with the United States Copyright Office. (Pl. Ex. 12 (Blair Decl.) at ¶ 4.) Although the market for the companion books is not nearly as large as the market for the Harry Potter series, Rowling's companion books have earned more than $30 million to date. (Tr. (Rowling) at 49:25-50:10; Pl. Ex. 25 (Rowling Decl.) at ¶ 6; Pl. Ex. 12 (Blair Decl.) at ¶ 3.)

Rowling has stated on a number of occasions since 1998 that, in addition to the two companion books, she plans to publish a "Harry Potter encyclopedia" after the completion of the series and again donate the proceeds to charity. (Tr. (Rowling) at 50:25-51: 15, 55: 1-5; Pl. Ex. 25 (Rowling Decl.) at ¶ 6; Pl. Ex. 12 (Blair Decl.) at ¶ 17.) Rowling intends that her encyclopedia contain alphabetical entries for the various people, places and things from the Harry Potter novels. (Tr. (Rowling) at 53:11-13.) While she intends to add new material as well, her encyclopedia is expected to reflect all of the information in the Harry Potter series. (Tr. (Vander Ark) at 387:20-388:16; Pl. Ex. 25 (Rowling Decl.) at ¶ 7; Pl. Ex. 32 (Suppl. Rowling Decl.) at ¶ 5.)

Rowling already has begun preparations for work on the encyclopedia by assembling her materials and requesting from her U.K. publisher its "bible" of Harry Potter materials. (Tr. (Rowling) at 52:1-24.) The publisher's "bible" is a catalogue of the people, places, and things from the Harry Potter books. (Pl. Ex. 23 (Odedina Decl.) ¶ 2; Pl. Ex. 23A.) Rowling's U.S. publisher has compiled a similar catalogue of elements from the Harry Potter books which Rowling has requested and intends to draw on in creating her encyclopedia. (Tr. (Rowling) at 52:25-53:10; Pl. Ex. 25 (Rowling Decl.) at ¶ 7; Pl. Ex. 18 (Klein Decl.) at ¶¶ 2-3; Pl. Ex. 18A.) Rowling plans on using an A-to-Z format for her encyclopedia. (Tr. (Rowling) at 53:11-13.)

## II. The Allegedly Infringing Work

Defendant RDR Books is a Michigan-based publishing company that seeks to publish a book entitled "The Lexicon," the subject of this lawsuit. (Tr. (Rapoport) at 150:19-151:2.) Steven Vander Ark, a former library media specialist at a middle school in Michigan (Tr. (Vander Ark) at 248:4-6), is the attributed author of the Lexicon (Def. Ex. 502 (Vander Ark Decl.) at ¶ 1). He is also the originator, owner, and operator of "The Harry Potter Lexicon" website (id.), a popular Harry Potter fan site from which the content of the Lexicon is drawn (id. at ¶ 30).

### A. The Origins of the Lexicon

An immediate fan of the Harry Potter novels, Vander Ark began taking personal notes to keep track of the details and elements that unfold in the Harry Potter world while reading the second book in the series in 1999. (Tr. (Vander Ark) at 335:2-17.) After joining an online discussion group about the Harry Potter books, Vander Ark expanded his notes to include descriptive lists of the spells, characters, and fictional objects in Harry Potter to share with fellow fans. (Id. at 335:20-336:9.) These lists included brief descriptions or definitions of the terms. (Id. at 336:8-11.)

Vander Ark began work on his website, "The Harry Potter Lexicon" (the "website" or "Lexicon website"), in 1999 and opened the website in 2000. (Id. at 336:23.) His purpose in establishing the website was to create an encyclopedia that collected and organized information from the Harry Potter books in one central source for fans to use for reference. (Id. at 338:6-21; Def. Ex. 502 (Vander Ark Decl.) at ¶ 13.) At its launch, the website featured Vander Ark's descriptive lists of spells, characters, creatures, and magical items from Harry Potter with hyperlinks to cross-referenced entries. (Tr. (Vander Ark) at 337:7-10, 336:4-7.) In response to feedback from users of the website, Vander Ark developed an A-to-Z index to each list to allow users to search for entries alphabetically. (Id. at 343:2-21.)

The website presently features several indexed lists of people, places, and things from Harry Potter, including the "Encyclopedia of Spells," "Encyclopedia of Potions," "Wizards, Witches, and Beings," "The Bestiary," and "Gazetteer of the Wizarding World." (Pl. Exs. 14 (Bradley Decl.) at ¶ 5, 14C.) In addition to these reference features, the website contains a variety of supplemental material pertaining to Harry Potter, including fan art, commentary, essays, timelines, forums, and interactive data. (Pl. Exs. 14 (Bradley Decl.) at ¶ 3, 14A.) The website is currently run by a staff of seven or eight volunteers, including four primary editors (Tr. (Vander Ark) at 340:14-16), all of whom were recruited to help update and expand the website's content after the publication of the fifth book in the Harry Potter series. (Id. at 339:18-340:24.) The website uses minimal advertising to offset the costs of operation. (Id. at 349:24-350:10.) Use of the website is free and unrestricted. (Id. at 293:8-12; 351:25-352:4.)

The content of the encyclopedia entries on the Lexicon website is drawn primarily from the Harry Potter series, the companion books, "The Daily Prophet" newsletters, the "Famous Wizard Cards," and published interviews of Rowling. (Tr. (Vander Ark) at 348:7-13; Def. Ex. 502 (Vander Ark Decl.) at ¶ 14). According to Vander Ark, some additional content is drawn from outside reference sources, including Bullfinch's Mythology, Field Guide to Little People, New Shorter Oxford English Dictionary, and online encyclopedias such as Encyclopedia Mythica. (Tr. (Vander Ark) at 346:12-348:19; Def. Ex. 502 (Vander Ark Decl.) at ¶ 14.) Frequently, these sources are not cited in the website's encyclopedia entries. Vander Ark's purpose in including additional information from outside sources or from his own knowledge was to enrich the experience of readers of the Harry Potter series by illuminating "the incredibly rich world and hidden meanings" contained within them. (Tr. (Vander Ark) at 345:21-346:6.)

Vander Ark has received positive feedback, including from Rowling and her publishers, about the value of the Lexicon website as a reference source. In May 2004, Vander Ark read a remark by Rowling posted on her website praising his Lexicon website as follows: "This is such a great site that I have been known to sneak into an internet café while out writing and check a fact rather than go into a bookshop and buy a copy of Harry Potter (which is embarrassing). A website for the dangerously obsessive; my natural home." (Tr. (Rowling) at 118:2-119:2). In July 2005, Vander Ark received a note from Cheryl Klein, a Senior Editor at Scholastic Inc., American publisher of the Harry Potter series, thanking him and his staff "for the wonderful resource [his] site provides for fans, students, and indeed editors & copyeditors of the Harry Potter series," who "referred to the Lexicon countless times during the editing of [the sixth book in the series], whether to verify a fact, check a timeline, or get a chapter & book reference for a particular event." (Def. Ex. 502 (Vander Ark Decl.) at ¶ 39; Def. Ex. 502A.) In September 2006, Vander Ark was invited by Warner Brothers to the set of the film The Order of the Phoenix, where he met David Heyman, the producer of all the Harry Potter films. Heyman told Vander Ark that Warner Brothers used the Lexicon website almost every day.[2] (Tr. 386:8-20; Def. Ex. 502 (Vander Ark Decl.) ¶ 39.) Finally, in July 2007, Vander Ark visited the studios of Electronic Arts, the licensed producer of the Harry Potter video games, where he observed printed pages from the Lexicon covering the walls of the studio. (Tr. at 387:3-13; Def. Ex. 502 (Vander Ark Decl.) ¶ 39.)

Prior to any discussions with RDR Books about publishing portions of the Lexicon website as a book, Vander Ark was aware of Rowling's public statements regarding her intention to write a Harry Potter encyclopedia upon completion of the seventh book in the series. (Tr. (Vander Ark) at 247:10-12, 250:21-251:13; Def. Ex. 502 at ¶ 37.) In June 2007, just before the release of the seventh book, Vander Ark emailed Christopher Little Literary Agency, Rowling's literary agent in the United Kingdom, and suggested that he would be "a good candidate for work as an editor, given [his] work on the Lexicon," should Rowling start working on an encyclopedia or other reference to the Harry Potter series. (Pl. Ex. 12C.) The literary agency advised him that Rowling

---

[2] This testimony was ruled admissible over Plaintiffs' hearsay objection for the purpose of showing that Vander Ark was told by Warner Brothers that it had used the Lexicon almost every day, and not for the truth of the statement. (Tr. at 386:24-387:1.) Regardless of whether or not Warner Brothers in fact used the Lexicon website every day during the production of the film, Vander Ark had reason to believe based on this statement that the website was serving its intended purpose as a reference guide to the Harry Potter novels.

intended to work alone and did not require a collaborator. (Tr. (Vander Ark) at 250:14-20; Pl. Ex. 12 (Blair Decl.) at ¶ 12; Pl. Ex. 12C.)

## B. RDR Books' Acquisition and Marketing of the Lexicon

Roger Rapoport is the president of Defendant RDR Books. Rapoport learned of Vander Ark and the Lexicon website when he read an article in his local newspaper dated July 23, 2007, profiling Vander Ark as a well known figure within the Harry Potter fan community and the proprietor of the Lexicon website who "holds the key to all things 'Harry Potter.'" (Tr. (Rapoport) at 153:2-154:15; Pl. Ex. 77.) Recognizing a publishing opportunity, Rapoport contacted Vander Ark on August 6, 2007 about the possibility of publishing a Harry Potter encyclopedia based on some of the materials from the Lexicon website. (Tr. (Vander Ark) at 357:10-19.) Rapoport denies seeing any coverage by national news outlets of Rowling's appearance on NBC's Today Show on July 25, 2007 (Tr. (Rapoport) at 156:10-158:4), where Rowling stated that she intended to write a Harry Potter encyclopedia. (Def. Ex. 506a; Tr. (Rapoport) at 155:20-156:5.)

At his first meeting with Rapoport in August 2007, Vander Ark raised his concerns regarding the permissibility of publishing the Lexicon in view of Rowling's plan to publish an encyclopedia and her copyrights in the Harry Potter books. (Tr. (Vander Ark) at 251:14-22, 358:2-4). Prior to August 2007, Vander Ark had developed and circulated the opinion that publishing "any book that is a guide to [the Harry Potter] world" would be a violation of Rowling's intellectual property rights. (Pl. Ex. 20 (Lares Decl.) at ¶ 3, Pl. Ex. 21 (Lawliss Decl.) at ¶ 3); see also Tr. (Vander Ark) at 251:20-22.) Vander Ark had even stated on a public internet newsgroup that he would not publish the Lexicon "in any form except online" without permission because Rowling, not he, was "entitled to that market." (Pl. Ex. 27 (Blumsack Corrected Supp. Decl.) at ¶ 12; Pl. Ex. 27G). Vander Ark changed his mind about publishing the Lexicon after Rapoport reassured him that he had looked into the legal issue and determined that publication of content from the Lexicon website in book form was legal. (Tr. (Vander Ark) at 357:10-359:5.) Rapoport agreed to stand by this opinion by adding an atypical clause to the publishing contract providing that RDR would defend and indemnify Vander Ark in the event of any lawsuits. (Tr. (Vander Ark) 359:6-10, 360:8-21; Def. Ex. 502 (Vander Ark Decl.) at ¶ 28; Pl. Ex. 14J.)

Rapoport and Vander Ark agreed that the content of the book would be limited to the encyclopedia sections of the Lexicon website that presented descriptions of the persons, places, spells, and creatures from the Harry Potter works. (Tr. (Vander Ark) at 359:14-21; Def. Ex. 502 (Vander Ark Decl.) at ¶ 28.) They conceived of the book as an encyclopedia organized in the A-to-Z format, rather than by topic as the Lexicon website is organized, to allow the user to find information as quickly as possible. (Tr. (Vander Ark) at 366:25-367:24.) The idea was to publish the first complete guide to the Harry Potter series that included information from the seventh and final Harry Potter novel. (Id. at 361:12-24.) Vander Ark believed that there was an advantage to being the first reference guide on the market to cover all seven Harry Potter books. (Id. at 255:7-14, 361:9-15). He also believed that by virtue of it completeness, the Lexicon would be most useful for the purpose it sought to serve, namely helping readers and fans to find information from the Harry Potter novels. (Id. at 361:17-362:6.)

RDR Books intended to have a manuscript of the Lexicon completed within two-to-three weeks of execution of the publishing contract. (Tr. (Vander Ark) at 255:15-18.)

The plan was to rush the book to market by late-October 2007, in part, to capitalize on the interest generated by the last Harry Potter book and the surge in sales during the holiday season. (Tr. (Rapoport) at 165:14-165:21, 167:10-17.) RDR Books initially planned a print-run of 10,000 copies of the Lexicon, but would undertake subsequent print-runs if the book was successful. (Tr. at (Rapoport) 238:22-239:20.)

Even before his initial meeting with Vander Ark, Rapoport began working to secure foreign publishers for the proposed Lexicon project and had contacted Methuen Publishing in the United Kingdom to gauge their interest in doing such a project. (Tr. (Rapoport) at 160:18-161:18.) He marketed the Lexicon to foreign publishers, as well as to U.S. bookstores and book sellers, as the "definitive" Harry Potter encyclopedia. (Tr. (Rapoport) at 160:18-161:15, 213:5-214:4; Tr. (Vander Ark) at 361:9-16; see also Pl. Exs. 114, 117.) Some of Rapoport's marketing communications mischaracterized Rowling's statements about the Lexicon website, giving the impression that she supported the publication of the Lexicon book. (Tr. at (Rapoport) 175:2-176:5; Pl. Ex. 89.) One marketing flyer for the Lexicon prominently displayed Rowling's 2004 statement praising the Lexicon website. (Tr. (Rapoport) at 171:3-6; Pl. Ex. 14 (Bradley Decl.) at ¶ 17; Pl. Ex. 22 (Murphy Decl.) at ¶ 15; Pl. Ex. 22A). As a result of Rapoport's marketing efforts, RDR Books secured oral contracts with foreign publishers for rights to the Lexicon in England, Canada, France, Australia, New Zealand, and China, and an order from Borders bookstore[3] in the United States. (Tr. (Rapoport) at 187:2-11; 240:15-241:4; Pl. Ex. 137).

---

[3] Rapoport admitted that Borders' order was cancelled because of the instant lawsuit. (Tr. (Rapoport) at 241:15-23).

## C. Plaintiffs' Objections to Publication of the Lexicon

Rowling's literary agent, Neil Blair of the Christopher Little Literary Agency, first learned of the Lexicon book when he saw an advertisement on www.PublishersMarketplace.com announcing that RDR Books would be publishing the Lexicon, scheduled for release in late October 2007. (Pl. Exs. 12 (Blair Decl.) at ¶ 14, 12D). On September 18, 2007, counsel for Rowling and Warner Brothers forwarded a letter to Vander Ark by email, copying Rapoport, notifying them that the Lexicon appeared to infringe Rowling's copyrights and requesting that RDR Books cease publication of the book. (Tr. at (Rapoport) 190:7-13; Pl. Ex. 15 at ¶ 3). Rapoport replied to Plaintiffs' counsel that he intended to study the various issues with RDR Books' legal advisers (Pl. Ex. 15 (Cendali Decl.) at ¶ 5) and that his work had been interrupted by personal circumstances (id. ¶ 7). Meanwhile he continued to market the Lexicon book domestically and abroad. (Tr. (Rapoport) at 193:2-25, 194:4-14, 208:3-17; Pl. Exs. 110-130, 133-140.)

On October 3, 2007, after receiving no substantive response from RDR Books, Plaintiffs' counsel wrote again to Rapoport emphasizing their clients' concerns and asking for a prompt substantive response. (Pl. Ex. 15 (Cendali Decl.) at ¶ 6.) On October 5, 2007, when pitching the Lexicon to a Brazilian publisher, Rapoport asked for confirmation that the agent would not speak with the local publisher of the Harry Potter novels about the Lexicon. (Pl. Ex. 120.) On October 8, 2007, despite having received a cease-and-desist letter and a subsequent letter from Plaintiffs' counsel, Rapoport told a German publisher who raised copyright concerns that a lawsuit was unlikely. (Tr. (Rapoport) at 198:6-19; Pl. Ex. 121.)

On October 11, 2007, RDR Books sent the chairman of Warner Brothers a cease-and-desist letter claiming that Warner Brothers had violated Vander Ark's rights in the "Hogwarts Timeline" of events from the Harry Potter novels that was featured on the Lexicon website. (Pl. Ex. 14 (Bradley Decl.) at ¶ 12; Pl. Ex. 14H). RDR Books also stated that it was seeking "tangible rewards" for Vander Ark in exchange for Warner Brothers' purported use of the timeline as an extra feature of the DVD versions of the first three Harry Potter films. (Id.) On October 19, 2007, Warner Brothers responded to RDR Books' letter regarding the timeline with a request for a copy of the "print version" of the Lexicon website referred to by RDR Books to aid its evaluation of any potential claims. (Pl. Ex. 15 (Cendali Decl.) at ¶¶ 8-9). RDR Books refused, stating that Warner Brothers could print the material from the Lexicon website. (Tr. (Rapoport) at 205:21-206:13; Pl. Ex. 15 (Cendali Decl.) at ¶ 9.)

On October 19 and 24, 2007, Plaintiffs' counsel sent two more letters to RDR Books, asking for a substantive response to their clients' concerns regarding the Lexicon and for confirmation that RDR Books would not publish the Lexicon until it attempted to resolve the matter in good faith. (Pl. Ex. 15 (Cendali Decl.) at ¶¶ 9, 11.) RDR Books' responses deflected the inquiries (id. ¶ 10) and stated that Plaintiffs' objections were "unwarranted" (id. ¶ 12). On October 31, 2007, Plaintiffs called Rapoport to offer a last chance to agree to cease publication, or at least delay publication, and to provide Plaintiffs with a copy of the manuscript and proposed cover, in effort to resolve the matter. (Id. ¶ 13.) RDR refused to delay publication and refused to provide a copy of the manuscript. (Id.) Plaintiffs filed suit on October 31, 2007, at which time they also moved by order to show cause for a preliminary injunction. (Id. ¶ 13; Compl.)

Since the filing of this lawsuit, RDR Books has revised the front and back covers of the Lexicon. Specifically, RDR Books removed the quotation of Rowling's 2004 statement about her use of the Lexicon website from the back cover of the Lexicon after Plaintiffs presented a survey in this litigation demonstrating that 38% of respondents believed that the appearance of the quote on the proposed book cover meant that Rowling endorsed the book. (Tr. (Rapoport) at 237:6-13; Pl. Ex. 13C (Blumsack Decl.); Pl. Ex. 16 (Helfgott Decl.) at ¶ 2). RDR Books changed the title from "The Harry Potter Lexicon" to "The Lexicon: An Unauthorized Guide to Harry Potter Fiction and Related Materials." Additionally, the final revision of the front cover of the Lexicon displays the following disclaimer:

> Harry Potter and the names of fictitious people and places in the Harry Potter novels are trademarks of Warner Bros. Entertainment, Inc. This book is not written, prepared, approved, or licensed by Warner Bros. Entertainment, Inc., Scholastic Corporation, Raincoast Books, Bloomsbury Publishing Plc, or J.K. Rowling, nor is the author, his staff members, www.HP-Lexicon.org or the publisher in any way affiliated with Warner Bros. Entertainment, Inc., Scholastic Corporation, Raincoast Books, Bloomsbury Publishing Plc, J.K. Rowling, or any other person or company claiming an interest in the Harry Potter works.

(Def. Ex. 501a.) RDR Books maintains, however, that the original cover was truthful and did not infringe any rights of Plaintiffs. (Def. Ex. 501 (Rapoport Decl.) at ¶ 6.)

**D. The Content of the Lexicon**

The Lexicon is an A-to-Z guide to the creatures, characters, objects, events, and places that exist in the world of Harry Potter. As received by the Court in evidence, the Lexicon manuscript is more than 400 type-written pages long and contains 2,437 entries organized alphabetically. The first few pages contain a list of abbreviations used throughout the Lexicon to cite to the original sources of the material.

The Lexicon manuscript was created using the encyclopedia entries from the Lexicon website. (Tr. (Vander Ark) at 365:1-5; Def. Ex. 502 (Vander Ark Decl.) ¶30.) Because of space limitations for the printed work, which seeks to be complete but also easy to use, about half of the material from the website was not included in the Lexicon manuscript. (Tr. 365:1-11, 366:9-18; Def. Ex. 502 (Vander Ark Decl.) ¶¶ 30, 31, 33.) The Lexicon itself makes clear that the only source of its content is the work of J.K. Rowling. The first page of the Lexicon manuscript states: "All the information in the Harry Potter Lexicon comes from J.K. Rowling, either in the novels, the 'schoolbooks,' from her interviews, or from material which she developed or wrote herself." (Pl. Ex. 1 at 1). While Vander Ark claims that the Lexicon uses material from outside reference sources, such as Bullfinch's Mythology, Field Guide to Little People, New Shorter Oxford English Dictionary, and online encyclopedias (Tr. (Vander Ark) at 346:12-348:19; Def. Ex. 502 (Vander Ark Decl.) at ¶ 14), it is not possible to confirm this claim because, aside from four dictionary citations, no other citations to third-party works appear in the Lexicon. (Tr. (Vander Ark) at 295:13-296:13).

The Lexicon entries cull every item and character that appears in the Harry Potter works, no matter if it plays a significant or insignificant role in the story. The entries cover every spell (e.g., Expecto Patronum, Expelliarmus, and Incendio), potion (e.g., Love Potion, Felix Felicis, and Draught of Living Death), magical item or device (e.g., Deathly Hallows, Horcrux, Cloak of Invisibility), form of magic (e.g., Legilimency, Occlumency, and the Dark Arts), creature (e.g., Blast-Ended Skrewt, Dementors, and Blood-Sucking Bugbears), character (e.g., Harry Potter, Hagrid, and Lord Voldemort), group or force (e.g., Aurors, Dumbledore's Army, Death Eaters), invented game (e.g.,

Quidditch), and imaginary place (e.g., Hogwarts School of Witchcraft and Wizardry, Diagon Alley, and the Ministry of Magic) that appear in the Harry Potter works. The Lexicon also contains entries for items that are not explicitly named in the Harry Potter works but which Vander Ark has identified, such as medical magic, candle magic, wizard space, wizard clothing, and remorse. Some of the entries describe places or things that exist in the real world but also have a place in the Harry Potter works, such as moors, Greece, and Cornwall.

Each entry, with the exception of the shortest ones, gathers and synthesizes pieces of information relating to its subject that appear scattered across the Harry Potter novels, the companion books, The Daily Prophet newsletters, Famous Wizard Cards, and published interviews of Rowling. The types of information contained in the entries include descriptions of the subject's attributes, role in the story, relationship to other characters or things, and events involving the subject. Repositories of such information, the entries seek to give as complete a picture as possible of each item or character in the Harry Potter world, many of which appear only sporadically throughout the series or in various sources of Harry Potter material.

The snippets of information in the entries are generally followed by citations in parentheses that indicate where they were found within the corpus of the Harry Potter works. The thoroughness of the Lexicon's citation, however, is not consistent; some entries contain very few citations in relation to the amount material provided. (See, e.g., Pl. Ex. 1, entry for "Dumbledore, Albus Percival Wulfric Brian" (containing no citations in a five-page entry); entry for "Granger, Hermione Jean" (containing no citations in a three-page entry); entry for "Chamber of Secrets" (containing one citation for nearly two pages of material); entry for "Crouch, Bartemius 'Barty', Sr." (containing one citation for nearly a full page of material).) When the Lexicon cites to one of the seven Harry Potter novels, the citation provides only the book and chapter number. Vander Ark explained that page numbers were excluded from the citations because the various editions of the Harry Potter books have different pagination, but the chapter numbers remain consistent. (Tr. (Vander Ark) at 277:19-278:1.) The Lexicon neither assigns a letter to each edition nor specifies a standard edition while providing a conversion table for other editions, practices which Plaintiffs' expert Jeri Johnson testified were common for reference guides. (Tr. (Johnson) at 594:11-16, 594:20-595:3.)

While not its primary purpose, the Lexicon includes commentary and background information from outside knowledge on occasion. For example, the Lexicon contains sporadic etymological references, (e.g., Pl. Ex. 1, entries for "Colloportus," "Lupin, Remus," "Alohamora," "Fidelius Charm"), analogies to characters outside the Harry Potter world such as Merlin, and observations of Rowling's allusions to other works of literature such as "the weird sisters" from Shakespeare's Macbeth. The Lexicon also points to the very few "flints," or errors in the continuity of the story, that appear in the Harry Potter series. (See Tr. (Vander Ark) at 297:15-298:4.)

While there was considerable opining at trial as to the type of reference work the Lexicon purports to be and whether it qualifies as such (no doubt in part due to its title), the Lexicon fits in the narrow genre of non-fiction reference guides to fictional works. As Defendant's expert testified, the Harry Potter series is a multi-volume work of fantasy literature, similar to the works of J.R.R. Tolkien and C.S. Lewis. Such works lend themselves to companion guides or reference works because they reveal an elaborate imaginary world over thousands of pages, involving many characters, creatures, and magical objects that appear and reappear across thousands of pages. (Tr. (Sorensen) at 504:16-23; id. at 507:1-5 (testifying that she found 19 or 20 companion guides to J.R.R. Tolkien's works, and about 15 guides to C.S. Lewis's works).) Fantasy literature spawns books having a wide variety of purposes and formats, as demonstrated by the books about Harry Potter that Plaintiffs entered into evidence. (Pl. Exs. 73, 74, 75, 192; 13E-13G.) The Lexicon, an A-to-Z guide which synthesizes information from the series and generally provides citations for location of that information rather than offering commentary, is most comparable to the comprehensive work of Paul F. Ford, Companion to Narnia: A Complete Guide to the Magical World of C.S. Lewis's The Chronicles of Narnia (Pl. Ex. 62), or the unauthorized A-to-Z guide by George W. Beahm, Fact, Fiction, and Folklore in Harry Potter's World: An Unofficial Guide (Pl. Ex. 192).[4]

At trial, Rowling testified that the Lexicon took "all the highlights of [her] work, in other words [her] characters' secret history, the jokes certainly, certain exciting narrative twists, all the things that are the highlights of [her] stories." (Tr. (Rowling) at 647:6-10). She compared this taking of her work to plundering all of the "plums in [her] cake." (Tr. (Rowling) at 647:3-6). At trial, the testimony of Rowling and the expert opinion of Johnson focused at length on the Lexicon's verbatim copying of language from the Harry Potter works. Johnson testified that in particular, entries that deal with invented terms, creatures, places and things from the Harry Potter books use "again and

---

[4] The Companion to Narnia, however, is far more erudite and informative than the Lexicon. The Harry Potter guide by Beahm does not provide citations for the sources of its information and is less comprehensive than the Lexicon in that it covers only certain categories of information (e.g., Fabulous Beasts, Wizards, Magical Spells, etc.).

again the specific, very colorful, idiosyncratic . . . nouns and phrases of Ms. Rowling."
(Tr. (Johnson) at 619:7-9.)

Although it is difficult to quantify how much of the language in the Lexicon is directly lifted from the Harry Potter novels and companion books,[5] the Lexicon indeed contains at least a troubling amount of direct quotation or close paraphrasing of Rowling's original language.[6] The Lexicon occasionally uses quotation marks to indicate Rowling's language, but more often the original language is copied without quotation marks, often making it difficult to know which words are Rowling's and which are Vander Ark's. (Tr. (Rowling) at 57:6-15, 58:24-59:12, 59:19-60:2; Tr. (Johnson) at 619:3-12.)

For example, in the entry for "armor, goblin made," the Lexicon uses Rowling's poetic language nearly verbatim without quotation marks.[7] The original language from Harry Potter and the Deathly Hallows reads:

> "Muggle-borns," he said. "Goblin-made armour does not require cleaning, simple girl. Goblins' silver repels mundane dirt, imbibing only that which strengthens it."

(Pl. Ex. 10 at 303.)[8] The Lexicon entry for "armor, goblin made" reads in its entirety:

---

[5] Rowling went so far as to say that "if Mr. Vander Ark had put quotation marks around everything he has lifted, most of the Lexicon would be in quotation marks." (Tr. (Rowling) at 64:19-21.)

[6] Some of the most extensive direct quotation occurs where the Lexicon reproduces a song or poem that appears in the novels, such as the "Hogwarts' School Song," the Sorting Hat Song, and the poem, "His Eyes are as Green as a Fresh Pickled Toad." (Pl. Ex. 11 (Birchall Decl.) at ¶ 8, Pl. Ex. 11E-11G.) During his testimony at trial, Vander Ark conceded that these entries took too much and offered to remove the poems and songs from the Lexicon. (Tr. (Vander Ark) at 397:1-3.) In its post-trial brief, Defendant acknowledged this testimony (Def. Post-trial Br. ¶ 51, at 17), but did not confirm that Vander Ark's proposal would be adopted by RDR Books.

[7] Italics are used in the block quotations to highlight the original language that is copied or paraphrased. The italics do not appear in the originals.

[8] Having determined that the charts introduced by Plaintiffs (Pl. Exs. 47, 48, 43, and 44) do not consistently represent the language from the Lexicon with accuracy, the Court relies not on the charts but on the underlying texts themselves for its comparisons.

>Some armor in the wizarding world is made by goblins, and it is quite valuable. (e.g.,HBP20) According to Phineas Nigellus, goblin-made armor does not require cleaning, because goblins' silver repels mundane dirt, imbibing only that which strengthens it, such as basilisk venom. In this context, "armor" also includes blades such as swords.

Although the Lexicon entry introduces Rowling's language with the phrase, "According to Phineas Nigellus," it does not use quotation marks.

The Lexicon entry for "Dementors" reproduces Rowling's vivid description of this creature sometimes using quotation marks and sometimes quoting or closely paraphrasing without indicating which language is original expression. The original language appears in Chapters 5 and 10 of <u>Harry Potter and the Prisoner of Azkaban</u> as follows:

> . . . Its face was completely hidden beneath its hood. . . . There was a hand protruding from the cloak and it was glistening, grayish, slimy-looking, and scabbed, like something dead that had decayed in water. . . .
> And then the thing beneath the hood, whatever it was, drew a long, slow, rattling breath, as though it were trying to suck something more than air from its surroundings.

> \* \* \*

> "Dementors are among the foulest creatures to walk this earth. They infest the darkest, filthiest places, they glory in decay and despair, they drain peace, hope, and happiness out of the air around them. Even Muggles feel their presence, though they can't see them. Get too near a dementor and every good feeling, every happy memory will be sucked out of you. If it can, the dementor will feed on you long enough to reduce you to something like itself . . . soulless and evil. . . ."

(Pl. Ex. 6 at 83, 187.) The Lexicon entry for "Dementors" reads in its entirety:

>Dementors are some of the most terrible creatures on earth, flying tall black spectral humanoid things with flowing robes. They "infest the darkest, filthiest places, they glory in decay and despair, they drain peace, hope, and happiness out of the air around them," according to Lupin (PA10). Dementors affect even Muggles, although Muggles can't see the foul, black creatures. Dementors feed on positive human emotions; a large crowd is like a feast to them. They drain a wizard of his power if left

with them too long. They were the guards at Azkaban and made that place horrible indeed. The Ministry used Dementors as guards in its courtrooms as well (GF30, DH13). There are certain defenses one can use against Dementors, specifically the Patronus Charm. A Dementor's breath sounds rattling and like it's trying to suck more than air out of a room. Its hands are "glistening, grayish, slimy-looking, and scabbed". It exudes a biting, soul-freezing cold (PA5).

Another example of verbatim copying and close paraphrase can be found in the Lexicon entry for "Mirror of Erised." The original language from Harry Potter and the Sorcerer's Stone reads:

> It was a magnificent mirror, as high as the ceiling, with an ornate gold frame, standing on two clawed feet. There was an inscription carved around the top: Erised stra ehru oyt ube cafru oyt on wohsi.
>
> * * *
>
> . . . "It shows us nothing more or less than the deepest desire of our hearts. You [Harry Potter], who have never known your family, see them standing around you. Ronald Weasley, who has always been overshadowed by his brothers, sees himself standing alone, the best of all of them. However, this mirror will give us neither knowledge or truth. Men have wasted away before it, entranced by what they have seen, or been driven mad, not knowing if what it shows is real or even possible."

(Pl. Ex. 4 at 207, 213). The first paragraph of the Lexicon entry reads:

> A magnificent mirror, as high as a classroom ceiling, with an ornate gold frame, standing on two clawed feet. The inscription carved around the top reads "Erised stra ehru oyt ube cafru oyt on wohsi," which is "I show you not your face but your heart's desire" written backwards (that is, in what is called 'mirror writing'). When you look into the mirror you see the deepest, most desperate desire of your heart. The mirror has trapped people who can't bear to stop staring into it, unsure if what they see is going to actually happen. Harry sees his family in the Mirror; Ron sees himself as Head Boy and Quidditch champion (PS12).

The Lexicon entry for "Boggart" takes strands of dialogue from Harry Potter and the Prisoner of Azkaban and closely paraphrases it in the third person. The original work contains the following bits of dialogue:

"Boggarts like dark, enclosed spaces."

> "It's a shape-shifter. . . . It can take the shape of whatever it thinks will frighten us most."
> "Nobody knows what a boggart looks like when he is alone, but when I let him out, he will immediately become whatever each of us most fears."

(Pl. Ex. 6 at 133.) The Lexicon entry begins as follows:

> A shape shifter that prefers to live in dark, confined spaces, taking the form of the thing most feared by the person it encounters; nobody knows what a boggart looks like in its natural state.

An example of particularly extensive direct quotation is found in the Lexicon entry for "Trelawney, Sibyll Patricia," the professor of Divination at the Hogwarts School who tells two important prophecies in the story. The Lexicon not only reproduces her prophecies word-for-word in their entirety, but in doing so, reveals dramatic plot twists and how they are resolved in the series. For example, the first prophecy reads:

> "The one with the power to vanquish the Dark Lord approaches. . . . Born to those who have thrice defied him, born as the seventh month dies . . . and the Dark Lord will mark him as his equal, but he will have power the Dark Lord knows not . . . and either must die at the hand of the other for neither can live while the other survives. . . . The one with the power to vanquish the Dark Lord will be born as the seventh month dies. . . ."

(Pl. Ex. 8 at 841 (ellipses in original).) The Lexicon entry reproduces this prophecy exactly but in italics and indented. (Pl. Ex. 1, entry for "Trelawney, Sibyll Patricia.") The Lexicon entry continues by discussing what happens as a result of this prophecy: "Severus Snape was eavesdropping on this conversation and he reported the first part of the Prophecy to the Dark Lord. Voldemort immediately began searching for this threat, and centered his attention on the child of Lily and James Potter. (OP 37)." The entry then quotes the second prophecy, but without a citation to where it appears in the <u>Harry Potter</u> series.

A number of Lexicon entries copy Rowling's artistic literary devices that contribute to her distinctive craft as a writer. For example, the Lexicon entry for "brain room," uses Rowling's evocative literary device in a very close paraphrase. The original language from Harry Potter and the Order of the Phoenix reads:

> For a moment it seemed suspended in midair, then it soared toward Ron, spinning as it came, and what looked like ribbons of moving images flew from it, unraveling like rolls of film.

(Pl. Ex. 8 at 798.) The Lexicon entry reads in part:

> . . . When Summoned, the brains fly out of the tank, unspooling ribbons of thought like strips of film, which wrap themselves around the Summoner and cause quite a bit of damage (OP35). . . .

The Lexicon entry for "Clankers" copies a vivid simile created by Rowling and reproduces a thought in the mind of Harry Potter as a factual statement using nearly identical wording. The original language from Harry Potter and the Deathly Hallows reads:

> Ron passed the bag to Griphook, and the goblin pulled out a number of small metal instruments that when shaken made a loud, ringing noise like miniature hammers on anvils. . . .
> . . . Harry could see [the dragon] trembling, and as they drew nearer he saw the scars made by vicious slashes across its face, and guessed that it had been taught to fear hot swords when it heard the sound of the Clankers.

(Pl. Ex. 10 at 536). The Lexicon entry reads:

> A number of small metal instruments, which when shaken make a loud, ringing noise like tiny hammers on anvil [sic]. Anyone visiting one of the high-security vaults at Gringotts must carry one of these, shaking it to make noise. The dragon guarding those vaults has been conditioned to back away at the sound, apparently by being taught to fear hot swords whenever it hears the Clankers (DH26).

Similarly, the Lexicon entry for "Marchbanks, Madam Griselda" uses an artful simile from the original works to describe this character. Rowling's language in Harry Potter and the Order of the Phoenix reads:

> . . . Harry thought Professor Marchbanks must be the tiny, stooped witch with a face so lined it looked as though it had been draped in cobwebs; Umbridge was speaking to her very deferentially. . . .

(Pl. Ex. 8 at 710.) The Lexicon entry reads in part:

> . . . Madam Marchbanks in June 1996 was tiny and stooped, her face so lined it appeared draped in cobwebs. . . .

The Lexicon's close paraphrasing is not limited to the seven Harry Potter novels, but can be found in entries drawn from the companion books as well. For example, the entry for "Montrose Magpies" uses language from Quidditch Through the Ages. The original language reads:

> The Magpies are the most successful team in the history of the British and Irish League, which they have won thirty-two times. Twice European Champions . . . . The Magpies wear black and white robes with one magpie on the chest and another on the back.

(Pl. Ex. 2 at 35-36.) The Lexicon entry reads:

> The most successful Quidditch team in history, which has won the British and Irish league thirty-two times and the European Cup twice. Their robes are black and white, with one magpie on the chest and another on the back (QA7).

(See also Pl. Ex. 1, entry for "Woollongong Shimmy.")

The same close paraphrasing takes place in the Lexicon entries drawing from Rowling's other companion book, Fantastic Beasts & Where to Find Them. For example, the entry for "Chinese Fireball" closely tracks the original language, which reads:

> The only Oriental dragon. Scarlet and smooth-scaled, it has a fringe of golden spikes around its snub-snouted face and extremely protuberant eyes. The Fireball gained its name for the mushroom-shaped flame that bursts from its nostrils when it is angered. . . . Eggs are a vivid crimson speckled with gold. . . .

(Pl. Ex. 3 at 11.) The Lexicon entry reads:

> A species of dragon native to China. The Fireball is a scarlet dragon with golden spikes around its face and protruding eyes. The blast of flame from a fireball forms a distinctive mushroom shape. Eggs of a Fireball are vivid crimson, flecked with gold (FB).

(See also Pl. Ex. 1, entry for "Fire Crab.")

Instances of such verbatim copying or close paraphrasing of language in the Harry Potter works occur throughout the Lexicon. (See, e.g., Pl. Ex. 1, entries for "Apparition," "Bubtotuber," "Pince, Madam Irma," "Twycross, Wilkie," "Lovegood, Luna," "third-floor corridor," "Slytherin common room.") Rowling provides numerous examples in Plaintiffs' Exhibit 47, "a chart [she] made to show what [she] felt was the constant pilfering of [her] work." (Tr. (Rowling) at 57:23-24.)

Aside from verbatim copying, another factual issue of contention at trial was the Lexicon entries that contain summaries of certain scenes or key events in the Harry Potter series. Most frequently, these are the longer entries that describe important objects, such as the "Deathly Hallows," or momentous events, such as the "Triwizard Tournament," or that trace the development of an important character, such as Harry Potter, Lord Voldemort, Severus Snape, and Albus Dumbledore. Plaintiffs' expert testified at length that in her opinion these entries constitute "plot summaries," (Tr. (Johnson) at 592:14-22, 611:13-22, 623:4-624:11), while Defendant's expert characterized them as character studies or analysis.

Neither of these characterizations is exactly apt. Without endorsing one characterization or another, such entries in the Lexicon do encapsulate elements of the very elaborate and wide ranging plot (sometimes in chronological order, sometimes not) confined to the subject of the entry. In the entries for significant characters, these plot elements are occasionally used to support an observation about the character's nature or development. For instance, the three-and-a-half page entry for "Lovegood, Luna" contains the following paragraph:

> Luna came into her own during her sixth year at Hogwarts. With Harry, Ron, and Hermione gone from school, she joined Ginny and Neville to revive the D.A. and resist the Death Eaters' influence at Hogwarts. She was kidnapped on the Hogwarts Express on her way home for the Christmas holidays (DH25) because of what Mr. Lovegood had been writing in The Quibbler, and imprisoned in the cellar at the Malfoy Mansion along with Ollivander. She was helpful in their efforts to escape the Malfoy Mansion, and then fought bravely, again, at the Battle of Hogwarts (DH31).

(See also, e.g., Pl. Ex. 1, entry for "Malfoy, Draco," ¶¶ 5, 6, 7.) But other times, the presentation of plot details, in effect, summarizes a vignette or portion of a scene. In the same entry for "Lovegood, Luna," the Lexicon summarizes a scene on the Hogwarts Express found on pages 185 to 188 of Chapter 10 of Harry Potter and the Order of the Phoenix:

> Harry met Luna for the first time aboard the Hogwarts Express on September 1, 1995. He, Ginny, and Neville shared a compartment with her on the train (OP10). She was reading a copy of The Quibbler magazine upside down. She informed the others that her father is the editor of The Quibbler, a magazine which most in the Wizarding World consider a joke. She laughed a little too loud; she stared at the other kids, and generally made an odd traveling companion. Harry privately thought, when Cho happened by their compartment to say hello, that he would much rather have been sitting with "cooler" kids than Luna and Neville.

(Compare Pl. Ex. 8 at 185-88.)

The entries for the hero and the villain of the Harry Potter series (Harry Potter and Lord Voldemort) present the closest thing to "plot summaries," but are more aptly characterized as synopses or outlines of the narrative revolving around those characters. Because Harry Potter and Lord Voldemort drive the narrative and because they appear in nearly every chapter of the series, an encapsulation of the events surrounding them ultimately yields a synopsis of the primary narrative thread in the Harry Potter series. The Lexicon entry for "Potter, Harry James" is eleven pages long and chronicles each year of Harry Potter's life at the fictional Hogwarts School, providing the reader with all of the main events of the story through all seven of Rowling's novels, leading up to Harry Potter's final battle with Lord Voldemort. (Pl. Ex. 11 (Birchall Decl.) at ¶ 5). The nine-page entry for "Voldemort, Lord" begins by providing the pre-story for the character, which is included in the sixth Harry Potter novel, giving background into the character as a child. (Tr. (Rowling) at 146:10-13). The entry then proceeds to describe chronologically all of the events surrounding this character in the Harry Potter story from books one through seven, and also gives an account of this character's death in the last Harry Potter novel. (Tr. (Rowling) at 62: 12-20; Tr. (Johnson) at 623:6-624:11). Although the entries proceed chronologically and do not use the same plot structure as do the Harry Potter novels (which structure the plot so as to create an interesting drama), the entries do provide a skeleton of the plot elements that hold the story together.

Finally, Plaintiffs established the Lexicon's extensive copying from Rowling's companion books, Quidditch Through the Ages and Fantastic Beasts & Where to Find Them, the schoolbooks used by the students attending the Hogwarts School. These two books are very short, fifty-six and fifty-nine pages,[9] respectively. They are written in non-narrative form (Tr. (Vander Ark) at 396:21-25) and present fictional facts without commentary (id. (Rowling) at 63:18-20), in a similar way to the Lexicon. When questioned about his use of these books in creating the Lexicon, Vander Ark testified:

> . . . Fantastic Beasts and Quidditch [Through] the Ages had sections of them which were essentially encyclopedias already which presented quite a problem. We wanted to be complete, but we certainly didn't want to replace Ms. Rowling's encyclopedia content which presented us with quite a challenge of how to do that, how to include information, but not to include all of it. And that was what we decided to do. We said we'll intentionally leave things out and put a very clear note, Please go read her books, which is what we did.

(Id. (Vander Ark) 287:20-288:4.) Although the Lexicon sporadically leaves out material, such as some material from the introductory chapters of Quidditch Through the Ages, it essentially takes wholesale from the companion books. (Tr. (Rowling) at 65:3-8, 62:25-63:1.) When questioned about the Lexicon entry for "Chudley Cannons" and whether there was anything about this quidditch team in Quidditch Through the Ages that he did not put in the Lexicon, Vander Ark admitted, "In that particular case, it looks like we pretty much caught it all." (Id. at 288:15-22.)[10] Vander Ark later admitted that although he left out some of the first half of Quidditch Through the Ages, "[w]hen it comes to

---

[9] Fantastic Beasts & Where to Find Them is fifty-nine pages including the introductory material.
[10] The passage describing the Chudley Cannons from Quidditch Through the Ages reads in full as follows:
> The Chudley Cannons' glory days may be considered by many to be over, but their devoted fans live in hope of a renaissance. The Cannons have won the League twenty-one times, but the last time they did so was in 1892 and their performance over the last century has been lackluster. The Chudley Cannons wear robes of bright orange emblazoned with a speeding cannon ball and a double "C" in black. The club motto was changed in 1972 from "We shall conquer' to "Let's all just keep our fingers crossed and hope for the best."

(Pl. Ex. 2 at 33-34.) The Lexicon entry for "Chudley Cannons" reads in part as follows:
> . . . The Cannons wear orange robes with a speeding black cannon ball and a double letter C on them. They hail from Chudley. The Cannons have won the league twenty-ojne [sic] times, but the last time was in 1892. As a result of this endless losing streak, the club motto, which used to be "We shall conquer", was changed in 1972 to 'Let's all just keep our fingers crossed and hope for the best (QA7). . . .

28

descriptions of specific things, a Quidditch f[oul], for example, there's not a lot of information there to condense, and so there would be more of that included and referenced." (Id. at 290:3-6.)[11] Similarly, the Lexicon copies a large part of the descriptions of each beast in the A-to-Z section of Fantastic Beasts & Where to Find Them.

**CONCLUSIONS OF LAW**

**I.  Copyright Infringement**

To establish a prima facie case of copyright infringement, a plaintiff must demonstrate "(1) ownership of a valid copyright, and (2) copying of constituent elements of the work that are original." Feist Publ'ns, Inc. v. Rural Tel. Serv. Co., 499 U.S. 340, 361 (1991); Arica Institute, Inc. v. Palmer, 970 F.2d 1067, 1072 (2d Cir. 1992). The element of copying has two components: first, the plaintiff must establish actual copying by either direct or indirect evidence; then, the plaintiff must establish that the copying amounts to an improper or unlawful appropriation. Castle Rock Entm't, Inc. v. Carol Publ'g Group, Inc., 150 F.3d 132, 137 (2d Cir. 1998); Laureyssens v. Idea Group, Inc., 964 F.2d 131, 139-140 (2d Cir. 1992). The plaintiff demonstrates that the copying is actionable "by showing that the second work bears a 'substantial similarity' to protected expression in the earlier work." Castle Rock, 150 F.3d at 137 (citing Repp v. Webber, 132 F.3d 882, 889 (2d Cir. 1997)); see Ringgold v. Black Entm't Television, Inc., 126 F.3d 70, 74-75 (explaining the distinction between actionable copying and factual

---

[11] Quidditch Through the Ages contains a chart of all the fouls in quidditch and their description. (Pl. Ex. 2, at 29-30.) The Lexicon reproduces the descriptions from this chart in the entries for each of the fouls.

copying); 4 Melville B. Nimmer & David Nimmer, Nimmer on Copyright § 13.03[A] (2007) [hereinafter Nimmer].

**A. Ownership**

There is no dispute regarding Plaintiff Rowling's ownership of valid copyrights in the seven Harry Potter novels and two companion books, Quidditch Through the Ages and Fantastic Beasts & Where to Find Them. With respect to those works, Plaintiffs introduced evidence of copyright ownership in the form of registration certificates from the U.S. Copyright Office (Pl. Ex. 12-A), which constitute prima facie evidence of the works' copyrightability and the validity of the copyrights. 17 U.S.C. § 410(c). Plaintiffs also introduced the declarations and testimony of Rowling concerning her creation of the works and ownership of the copyrights in them. (Pl. Exs. 25, 32; Tr. (Rowling) at 43:8-9.)

Defendant disputes, however, that Plaintiffs have established Rowling's ownership of copyrights in "The Daily Prophet" newsletters and Warner Brothers' beneficial ownership of copyrights in the Harry Potter video games that contain the allegedly infringed "Famous Wizard Cards." The only evidence offered at trial to establish Plaintiffs' ownership of these copyrights was Rowling's testimony. Plaintiffs attached to their post-trial brief documents demonstrating Rowling's U.K. copyright in the "The Daily Prophet" (Pl. Post-Trial Br., Ex. A) and Warner Brothers' joint ownership with Electronic Arts Inc. of U.S. copyrights in Harry Potter videogames (id., Ex. B). Having taken judicial notice of these documents as public records as permitted by the Federal Rules of Evidence, see Fed. R. Evid. 201(b)(2); Island Software & Computer Serv. v. Microsoft Corp., 413 F.3d 257, 261 (2d Cir. 2005), the Court concludes that

Plaintiffs have established ownership of copyrights in "The Daily Prophet" and the "Famous Wizard Cards." Plaintiffs cannot establish infringement of these works, however, because neither work was entered into evidence,[12] and they are not before the Court. Accordingly, Plaintiffs' claims of copyright infringement will be addressed only with respect to the seven Harry Potter novels and two companion guides.

**B. Copying**

There is no dispute that the Lexicon actually copied from Rowling's copyrighted works. Vander Ark openly admitted that he created and updated the content of the Lexicon by taking notes while reading the Harry Potter books and by using without authorization scanned, electronic copies of the Harry Potter novels and companion books. (Tr. (Vander Ark) at 335:9-17, 259:5-9, 16-23.) While acknowledging actual copying, Defendant disputes that the copying amounts to an improper or unlawful appropriation of Rowling's works. Defendant argues that Plaintiffs fail to establish a prima facie case of infringement because they have not shown that the Lexicon is substantially similar to the Harry Potter works.

The appropriate inquiry under the substantial similarity test is whether "the copying is quantitatively and qualitatively sufficient to support the legal conclusion that infringement (actionable copying) has occurred."[13] Ringgold, 126 F.3d at 75; accord Nihon Keizai Shimbun, Inc. v. Comline Bus. Data, Inc., 166 F.3d 65, 70 (2d Cir. 1999);

---

[12] At trial, Exhibits 45 and 46, which contain charts comparing text from the Famous Wizard Cards and The Daily Prophet with text from the Lexicon, were admitted as demonstrative exhibits, but the underlying works were not introduced.

[13] The post-trial briefs of the parties both suggest that Ringgold's quantitative/qualitative approach is the applicable test for substantial similarity in this case, and the Court agrees. Since the original and secondary works are of different genres, the question of substantial similarity is difficult to examine using the other tests applied in this Circuit. See Castle Rock, 150 F.3d at 139 ("Because in the instant case the original and secondary works are of different genres and to a lesser extent because they are in different media, tests for substantial similarity other than the quantitative/qualitative approach are not particularly helpful to our analysis.").

Castle Rock, 150 F.3d at 138. The quantitative component addresses the amount of the copyrighted work that is copied, while the qualitative component addresses the copying of protected expression, as opposed to unprotected ideas or facts. Ringgold, 126 F.3d at 75.

In evaluating the quantitative extent of copying in the substantial similarity analysis, the Court "considers the amount of copying not only of direct quotations and close paraphrasing, but also of all other protectable expression in the original work." Castle Rock, 150 F.3d at 140 n.6. As the Second Circuit has instructed, "[i]t is not possible to determine infringement through a simple word count," which in this case would be an insuperable task; "the quantitative analysis of two works must always occur in the shadow of their qualitative nature." Nihon Keizai, 166 F.3d at 71. Where, as here, the copyrighted work is "wholly original," rather than mixed with unprotected elements, a lower quantity of copying will support a finding of substantial similarity. Nihon Keizai, 166 F.3d at 71.

Plaintiffs have shown that the Lexicon copies a sufficient quantity of the Harry Potter series[14] to support a finding of substantial similarity between the Lexicon and Rowling's novels. The Lexicon draws 450 manuscript pages worth of material primarily from the 4,100-page Harry Potter series.[15] Most of the Lexicon's 2,437 entries contain

---

[14] The Court analyzes the amount of expression copied from the Harry Potter series in the aggregate, rather than from each individual novel in the series, following the Second Circuit's reasoning in Castle Rock, 150 F.3d at 138 (observing that "[o]ur precedents . . . tend to support the aggregate analysis," and resolving to "treat Seinfeld—a discrete, continuous television series—as a single work"). Cautioning against the aggregate approach used in Castle Rock, the Nimmer treatise warns that the "broader the series, the more all-encompassing plaintiff's copyright becomes, thereby squelching new expression in direct defiance to copyright's mandate of stimulating the production of new works." 4 Nimmer § 13.03[A][3]. In this case, however, because the Harry Potter novels tell one coherent narrative in a series, rather than tell discrete tales, the danger identified by Nimmer is less likely to exist.

[15] Not included in the Court's quantitative analysis is the small amount of information appearing in these 450 pages that is taken from other sources, common knowledge, or Vander Ark's contribution.

direct quotations or paraphrases, plot details, or summaries of scenes from one or more of the Harry Potter novels. As Defendant admits, "the Lexicon reports thousands of fictional facts from the Harry Potter works." (Def.'s Post-trial Br. at 35). Although hundreds pages or thousands of fictional facts may amount to only a fraction of the seven-book series, this quantum of copying is sufficient to support a finding of substantial similarity where the copied expression is entirely the product of the original author's imagination and creation. See Castle Rock, 150 F.3d at 138 (concluding that a Seinfeld trivia book that copied 643 fragments from 84 copyrighted Seinfeld episodes "plainly crossed the quantitative copying threshold under Ringgold"); Twin Peaks Prods., Inc. v. Publ'ns Int'l, Ltd., 996 F.2d 1366, 1372 (2d Cir. 1993) (upholding the district court's conclusion that "the identity of 89 lines of dialogue" between Twin Peaks teleplays and a guide to the television series constituted substantial similarity); see also Harper & Row, 471 U.S. at 548-49 (stating that "lifting verbatim quotes of the author's original language totaling between 300 and 400 words and constituting some 13% of [the defendant's] article" was sufficient to constitute copyright infringement).

The quantitative extent of the Lexicon's copying is even more substantial with respect to Fantastic Beasts and Quidditch Through the Ages. Rowling's companion books are only fifty-nine and fifty-six pages long, respectively. The Lexicon reproduces a substantial portion of their content, with only sporadic omissions, across hundreds of entries. (Tr. (Vander Ark) at 287:20-288:4 (testifying that to overcome the problem of copying the companion books, "which were essentially encyclopedias already," in their entirety, the Lexicon intentionally leaves some things out).

As to the qualitative component of the substantial similarity analysis, Plaintiffs have shown that the Lexicon draws its content from creative, original expression in the Harry Potter series and companion books. Each of the 2,437 entries in the Lexicon contains "fictional facts" created by Rowling, such as the attributes of imaginary creatures and objects, the traits and undertakings of major and minor characters, and the events surrounding them. The entry for "Boggart," for example, contains the fictional facts that a boggart is "[a] shape shifter that prefers to live in dark, confined spaces, taking the form of the thing most feared by the person it encounters; nobody knows what a boggart looks like in its natural state," and that "Lupin taught his third year Defence Against the Dark Arts class to fight [a boggart] with the Riddikulus spell (PA7), and used a boggart as a substitute for a Dementor in tutoring Harry (PA12)." (Pl. Ex. 1.) In Castle Rock Entertainment, Inc. v. Carol Publishing Group, Inc., the Second Circuit explained that such invented facts constitute creative expression protected by copyright because "characters and events spring from the imagination of [the original] authors." 150 F.3d at 139; see also Paramount Pictures Corp. v. Carol Publ'g Group, 11 F. Supp. 2d 329, 333 (S.D.N.Y. 1998) (stating that "[t]he characters, plots and dramatic episodes" that comprise the story of the "fictitious history of Star Trek" are the story's "original elements," protected by copyright). The Castle Rock court held that a trivia book which tested the reader's knowledge of "facts" from the Seinfeld series copied protected expression because "each 'fact' tested by [the trivia book] is in reality fictitious expression created by Seinfeld's authors." Id. It follows that the same qualitative conclusion should be drawn here, where each "fact" reported by the Lexicon is actually expression invented by Rowling.

Seeking to distinguish Castle Rock, Defendant argues that the qualitative similarity between the Lexicon and the Harry Potter works is significantly diminished because "the Lexicon uses fictional facts primarily in their factual capacity" to "report information and where to find it," unlike the Seinfeld trivia book, which used fictional facts "primarily in their fictional capacity to entertain and 'satisfy' the reader's 'craving' for the Seinfeld television series." (Def. Post-trial Br. at 36 (quoting Castle Rock, 150 F.3d at 142-43).) While this distinction is important, Defendant's argument goes to the fair use question of whether the Lexicon's use has a transformative purpose, not to the infringement question of whether the Lexicon, on its face, bears a substantial similarity to the Harry Potter works. The court in Castle Rock addressed these two inquires separately and found that the Seinfeld trivia book not only bore a substantial similarity to the Seinfeld series but also lacked a transformative purpose. See Castle Rock, 150 F.3d at 138-39, 141-43. What matters at the infringement stage of this case is that the copied text is expression original to Rowling, not fact or idea, and therefore is presumptively entitled to copyright protection. See Harper & Row, 471 U.S. at 547; Feist, 499 U.S. at 344-46. Even if expression is or can be used in its "factual capacity," it does not follow that expression thereby takes on the status of fact and loses its copyrightability.

Defendant also argues that while a substantial similarity may be found where invented facts are "reported and arranged in such a way as to tell essentially the same story" as the original, "the order in which the fictional facts are presented in the Lexicon bears almost no resemblance to the order in which the fictional facts are arranged to create the story of Harry Potter and the universe he inhabits." (Def. Post-trial Br. at 34, 36). Reproducing original expression in fragments or in a different order, however, does not preclude a finding of substantial similarity. See Castle Rock, 150 F.3d at 139 (finding a substantial similarity even though the allegedly infringing trivia book rearranged fragments of expression from Seinfeld in question-and-answer format); Paramount Pictures, 11 F. Supp. 2d at 333-34 (finding that a book containing brief synopses of major plot lines, histories of major characters, and descriptions of fictional alien species in Star Trek was substantially similar to the Star Trek series even though "the fictitious history is presented in a different order than that in which it appeared in the [original works]"). Regardless of how the original expression is copied, "'the standard for determining copyright infringement is not whether the original could be recreated from the allegedly infringing copy, but whether the latter is "substantially similar" to the former.'" Castle Rock, 150 F.3d at 141 (quoting Horgan v. Macmillan, Inc., 789 F.2d 157, 162 (2d Cir. 1986)). Here, the Lexicon's rearrangement of Rowling's fictional facts does not alter the protected expression such that the Lexicon ceases to be substantially similar to the original works.[16]

Furthermore, the law in this Circuit is clear that "the concept of similarity embraces not only global similarities in structure and sequence, but localized similarity in language." Twin Peaks, 996 F.2d at 1372 (endorsing the taxonomy of "comprehensive nonliteral similarity" and "fragmented literal similarity" from the Nimmer treatise, 4 Nimmer § 13.03[A][2]); see also Ringgold, 126 F.3d at 75 n.3; Arica Institute, 970 F.2d at 1073. In evaluating fragmented literal similarity, or "localized similarity in language," the Court examines the copying of direct quotations or close paraphrasing of the original

---

[16] Moreover, the Lexicon's arrangement of fictional facts, although far more extensive, is not so different from that of Fantastic Beasts, which organizes descriptions of creatures in alphabetical order, and Quidditch Through the Ages, which contains individual descriptions of quidditch fouls, teams, and countries where quidditch is played.

work. Castle Rock, 150 F.3d at 140; Paramount Pictures, 11 F. Supp. 2d at 333 ("Fragmented similarity refers to exact copying of a portion of a work."). As determined in the Findings of Fact, the Lexicon contains a considerable number of direct quotations (often without quotation marks) and close paraphrases of vivid passages in the Harry Potter works. Although in these instances, the Lexicon often changes a few words from the original or rewrites original dialogue in the third person, the language is nonetheless substantially similar. See Salinger v. Random House, Inc., 811 F.2d 90, 97 (2d Cir. 1987) (indicating that protected expression is infringed whether it is "quoted verbatim or only paraphrased"); Craft v. Kobler, 667 F. Supp. 120, 124 (S.D.N.Y. 1987) (stating that protected writing is infringed by "direct quotation" or "by paraphrase which remains sufficiently close that, in spite of changes, it appropriates the craft of authorship of the original"); see also 4 Nimmer § 13.03[A][1] ("The mere fact that the defendant has paraphrased rather than literally copied will not preclude a finding of substantial similarity. Copyright 'cannot be limited literally to the text, else a plagiarist would escape by immaterial variations.'" (footnote omitted) (quoting Nichols v. Universal Pictures Co., 45 F.2d 119, 121 (2d Cir. 1930))).

Notwithstanding the dissimilarity in the overall structure of the Lexicon and the original works, some of the Lexicon entries contain summaries of certain scenes or key events in the Harry Potter series, as stated in the Findings of Fact. These passages, in effect, retell small portions of the novels, though without the same dramatic effect. In addition, the entries for Harry Potter and Lord Voldemort give a skeleton of the major plot elements of the Harry Potter series, again without the same dramatic effect or structure. Together these portions of the Lexicon support a finding of substantial similarity. To be sure, this case is different from Twin Peaks, where forty-six pages of the third chapter of a guidebook to the Twin Peaks television series were found to constitute "essentially a detailed recounting of the first eight episodes of the series. Every intricate plot twist and element of character development appear[ed] in the Book in the same sequence as in the teleplays." 996 F.2d at 1372-73 (supporting the Second Circuit's finding of comprehensive nonliteral similarity). Those "plot summaries" were far more detailed, comprehensive, and parallel to the original episodes than the so-called "plot summaries" in this case. Nonetheless, it is clear that the plotlines and scenes encapsulated in the Lexicon are appropriated from the original copyrighted works. See Paramount Pictures, F. Supp. 2d at 334 (noting that Twin Peaks was distinguishable but nonetheless applying its broader holding that "a book which tells the story of a copyrighted television series infringes on its copyright"). Under these circumstances, Plaintiffs have established a prima facie case of infringement.

**C. Derivative Work**

Plaintiffs allege that the Lexicon not only violates their right of reproduction, but also their right to control the production of derivative works. The Copyright Act defines a "derivative work" as "a work based upon one or more preexisting works, such as a translation, musical arrangement, dramatization, fictionalization, motion picture version, sound recording, art reproduction, abridgment, condensation, or any other form in which a work may be *recast, transformed, or adapted*." 17 U.S.C. § 101 (emphasis added). A work "consisting of editorial revisions, annotations, elaborations, or other modifications which, as a whole, represents an original work of authorship" is also a derivative work. Id.

A work is not derivative, however, simply because it is "based upon" the preexisting works.[17] If that were the standard, then parodies and book reviews would fall under the definition, and certainly "ownership of copyright does not confer a legal right to control public evaluation of the copyrighted work." Ty, Inc. v. Publ'ns Int'l Ltd., 292 F.3d 512, 521 (7th Cir. 2002). The statutory language seeks to protect works that are "recast, transformed, or adapted" into another medium, mode, language, or revised version, while still representing the "original work of authorship." See Castle Rock, 150 F.3d at 143 n.9 (stating that "derivative works that are subject to the author's copyright transform an original work into a new mode of presentation"); Twin Peaks, 996 F.2d at 1373 (finding a derivative work where a guidebook based on the Twin Peak television series "contain[ed] a substantial amount of material from the teleplays, transformed from one medium to another"). Thus in Ty, Inc. v. Publications International Ltd., Judge Posner concluded, as the parties had stipulated, that a collectors' guide to Beanie Babies was not a derivative work because "guides don't *recast, transform, or adapt* the things to which they are guides." 292 F.3d at 520 (emphasis added).

Plaintiffs argue that based on the Twin Peaks decision "companion guides constitute derivative works where, as is the case here, they 'contain a substantial amount of material from [the underlying work.'" (Pl. Post-trial Br. ¶ 288, at 88-89.) This argument inaccurately states the holding of Twin Peaks and overlooks two important distinctions between the Lexicon and the guidebook in Twin Peaks. First, as mentioned earlier, the portions of the Lexicon that encapsulate plot elements or sketch plotlines bear

---

[17] The law in this Circuit has recognized that "even when one work is 'based upon' another, 'if the secondary work sufficiently transforms the expression of the original work such that the two works cease to be substantially similar, then the secondary work is not a derivative work and, for that matter, does not infringe the copyright of the original work.'" Well-Made Toy Mfg. Corp. v. Goffa Int'l Corp., 354 F.3d 112, 117 (2d Cir. 2003) (quoting Castle Rock, 150 F.3d at 143 n.9).

no comparison with the guidebook in Twin Peaks, whose plot summaries giving "elaborate recounting of plot details" were found to constitute an "abridgement" of the original work. See Twin Peaks, 996 F.2d at 1373 n.2 (reproducing an excerpt of the infringing book containing a high degree of detail). Given that the Lexicon's use of plot elements is far from an "elaborate recounting" and does not follow the same plot structure as the Harry Potter novels, Plaintiffs' suggestion that these portions of the Lexicon are "unauthorized abridgements" is unpersuasive. Second, and more importantly, although the Lexicon "contain[s] a substantial amount of material" from the Harry Potter works, the material is not merely "transformed from one medium to another," as was the case in Twin Peaks. Id. at 1373. By condensing, synthesizing, and reorganizing the preexisting material in an A-to-Z reference guide, the Lexicon does not recast the material in another medium to retell the story of Harry Potter, but instead gives the copyrighted material another purpose.[18] That purpose is to give the reader a ready understanding of individual elements in the elaborate world of Harry Potter that appear in voluminous and diverse sources. As a result, the Lexicon no longer "represents [the] original work[s] of authorship." 17 U.S.C. § 101. Under these circumstances, and because the Lexicon does not fall under any example of derivative works listed in the statute, Plaintiffs have failed to show that the Lexicon is a derivative work.

## II.  Fair Use

---

[18] This distinction is critical to the difference between derivative works, which are infringing, and works of fair use, which are permissible. See Castle Rock, 150 F.3d at 143 ("Although derivative works that are subject to the author's copyright transform an original work into a new mode of presentation, such works—unlike works of fair use—take expression for purposes that are not "transformative."); Twin Peaks, 996 F.2d at 1375-76 (suggesting that whether an abridgement is a fair use rather than a derivative work may depend on whether it serves "a transformative function and elaborates in detail far beyond what is required to serve any legitimate purpose"). But see Blanch v. Koons, 467 F.3d 244, 252 n.4 ("A derivative use can certainly be complementary to, or fulfill a different function from, the original.").

Defendant contends that even if Plaintiffs have shown a prima facie case of infringement, the Lexicon is nevertheless a fair use of the Harry Potter works. An integral part of copyright law, the fair use doctrine is designed to "fulfill copyright's very purpose, 'To promote the Progress of Science and useful Arts,'" Campbell v. Acuff-Rose Music, Inc., 510 U.S. 569, 575 (1994) (quoting U.S. Const. art. I, § 8, cl. 8), by balancing the simultaneous needs "to protect copyrighted material and to allow others to build upon it." Id. As the Second Circuit has observed, there is an

> inevitable tension between the property rights [that copyright law] establishes in creative works, which must be protected up to a point, and the ability of authors, artists, and the rest of us to express them– or ourselves by reference to the works of others, which must be protected up to a point. The fair-use doctrine mediates between the two sets of interests, determining where each set of interests ceases to control.

Blanch v. Koons, 467 F.3d 244, 250 (2d Cir. 2006). At stake in this case are the incentive to create original works which copyright protection fosters and the freedom to produce secondary works which monopoly protection of copyright stifles—both interests benefit the public. See Pierre N. Leval, Toward a Fair Use Standard, 103 Harv. L. Rev. 1105, 1109 (1990) (noting that on one hand "[t]he monopoly created by copyright . . . rewards the individual author in order to benefit the public," and on the other "[m]onopoly protection of intellectual property that impeded referential analysis and the development of new ideas out of old would strangle the creative process").

The common law doctrine of fair use is codified at Section 107 of the Copyright Act of 1976 as follows:

> The fair use of a copyrighted work . . . for purposes such as criticism, comment, news reporting, teaching (including multiple copies for classroom use), scholarship, or research, is not an infringement of copyright. In determining whether the use made of a work in any particular case is a fair use the factors to be considered shall include—

(1) the purpose and character of the use, including whether such use is of a commercial nature or is for nonprofit educational purposes;

(2) the nature of the copyrighted work;

(3) the amount and substantiality of the portion used in relation to the copyrighted work as a whole, and

(4) the effect of the use upon the potential market for or value of the copyrighted work.

17 U.S.C. § 107. The evaluation of these factors is "an open-ended and context-sensitive inquiry," Blanch, 467 F.3d at 244; accord Campbell, 510 U.S. at 577 (stating that "the statute, like the doctrine it recognizes, calls for a case-by-case analysis"), and the examples listed in the statute (i.e., criticism, comment, news reporting, and teaching) are illustrative rather than limiting, Campbell, 510 U.S. at 577-78. The four statutory factors may not "be treated in isolation, one from another"; instead they all must "be explored, and the results weighed together, in light of the purposes of copyright." Id. at 578. "The ultimate test of fair use, therefore, is whether the copyright law's goal of 'promoting the Progress of Science and useful Arts,' U.S. Const., art. I, § 8, cl. 8, 'would be better served by allowing the use than by preventing it.'" Castle Rock, 150 F.3d at 141 (quoting Arica Inst., 970 F.2d at 1077).

### A. Purpose and Character of the Use

Most critical to the inquiry under the first fair-use factor is "whether and to what extent the new work is 'transformative.'" Campbell, 510 U.S. at 579; see also Bill Graham Archives v. Dorling Kindersley Ltd, 448 F.3d 605, 608 (2d Cir. 2006); Elvis Presley Enters., Inc. v. Passport Video, 349 F.3d 622, 628 (9th Cir. 2003). Specifically, the court asks "whether the new work merely 'supersede[s] the objects' of the original creation, or instead adds something new, with a further purpose or different character, altering the first with new expression, meaning, or message." Campbell, 510 U.S. at 579. The fair use doctrine seeks to protect a secondary work if it "adds value to the original—if [copyrightable expression in the original work] is used as raw material, transformed in the creation of new information, new aesthetics, new insights and understandings," because such a work contributes to the enrichment of society. Castle Rock, 150 F.3d at 141 (alteration in original) (quoting Leval, supra, at 1111). Courts have found a transformative purpose both where the defendant combines copyrighted expression with original expression to produce a new creative work, see, e.g., Campbell, 510 U.S. at 582-83; Blanch, 467 F.3d at 251-51; Suntrust Bank v. Houghton Mifflin Co., 268 F.3d 1257 (11th Cir. 2001), and where the defendant uses a copyrighted work in a different context to serve a different function than the original, see, e.g., Perfect 10, Inc. v. Amazon.com, Inc., 508 F.3d 1146 (9th Cir. 2007); Bill Graham Archives v. Dorling Kindersley Ltd., 448 F.3d 605 (2d Cir. 2006).

The purpose of the Lexicon's use of the Harry Potter series is transformative. Presumably, Rowling created the Harry Potter series for the expressive purpose of telling an entertaining and thought provoking story centered on the character Harry Potter and set in a magical world. The Lexicon, on the other hand, uses material from the series for the practical purpose of making information about the intricate world of Harry Potter readily accessible to readers in a reference guide. To fulfill this function, the Lexicon identifies more than 2,400 elements from the Harry Potter world, extracts and synthesizes fictional facts related to each element from all seven novels, and presents that information in a format that allows readers to access it quickly as they make their way through the series. Because it serves these reference purposes, rather than the entertainment or aesthetic purposes of the original works, the Lexicon's use is transformative and does not supplant the objects of the Harry Potter works. See Elvis Presley Enters., 349 F.3d at 629 (stating that new works are described as transformative "when the works use copyrighted materials for purposes distinct from the purpose of the original material"); see also Bill Graham Archives, 448 F.3d at 609 (concluding that the use of artistic images as historical artifacts is "transformatively different from the original expressive purpose").

The Lexicon's use of Rowling's companion books, however, is transformative to a much lesser extent. Although there is no supporting testimony, the companion books can be used for a reference purpose. Their packaging demonstrates an entertainment purpose: bringing to life the fictional schoolbooks they represent in the Harry Potter novels, the companion books have fictional authors, forewords written by Albus Dumbledore, handwritten notes to Harry from his friends, a game of tic-tac-toe sketched on one page, a library log and warning by the Hogwarts librarian, and a "Property of Hogwarts Library" stamp. In this regard, the companion books serve as playful accessories to the Harry Potter series. At the same time, the content of the companion books takes on the informational purpose of the schoolbooks they represent in the novels. As Vander Ark testified, the companion books are "essentially encyclopedias already." (Tr. (Vander Ark) at 287:21-22.) Fantastic Beasts describes the attributes and origins of each beast listed in the alphabetical guide, defines "beast," and explains the place of beasts in the "muggle" and wizard worlds. Quidditch Through the Ages describes the history and development of quidditch, the rules of the game, the teams, and the spread of quidditch internationally. Neither book, however, makes reference to where the beasts or quidditch facts appear in the Harry Potter novels. Although the Lexicon does not use the companion books for their entertainment purpose, it supplants the informational purpose of the original works by seeking to relate the same fictional facts in the same way. Even so, the Lexicon's use is slightly transformative in that it adds a productive purpose to the original material by synthesizing it within a complete reference guide that refers readers to where information can be found in a diversity of sources.

The best evidence of the Lexicon's transformative purpose is its demonstrated value as a reference source. See Am. Geophysical Union v. Texaco Inc., 60 F.3d 913, (2d Cir. 1994) (stating that the "transformative use concept assesses the value generated by the secondary use and the means by which such value is generated"); Leval, supra, at 1111 (stating that for a use to be transformative, "[t]he use must be productive and must employ the quoted matter in a different manner or for a different purpose than the original"). The utility of the Lexicon, as a reference guide to a multi-volume work of fantasy literature, demonstrates a productive use for a different purpose than the original works. The Lexicon makes the elaborate imaginary world of Harry Potter searchable, item by item, and gives readers a complete picture of each item that cannot be gleaned by reading the voluminous series, since the material related to each item is scattered over thousands of pages of complex narrative and plot. The demand for and usefulness of this type of reference guide is evidenced by the publication of similar works such as Paul F. Ford's Companion to Narnia: A Complete Guide to the Magical World of C.S. Lewis's The Chronicles of Narnia. (Pl. Ex. 62; see also Def. Ex. 503 (Sorensen Decl.) ¶ 12.) The utility of the Lexicon as a reference guide has been demonstrated to Vander Ark by way of responses to his Lexicon website. This feedback included a remark by Rowling that she has "been known to sneak into an internet café while out writing and check a fact" on the Lexicon website, a remark by David Heyman of Warner Brothers that he used the Lexicon website almost every day while shooting the fifth Harry Potter film, and a glimpse of the walls of the Electronic Arts studios covered with printed pages from the Lexicon website. (Tr. 386:8-20, 387:3-13; Def. Ex. 502 (Vander Ark Decl.) ¶ 39.) This feedback supports Defendant's claim that it had good reason to believe that a print version of the Lexicon would serve as a valuable reference source to readers and fans of Harry Potter.

Its function as a reference guide distinguishes the Lexicon from the secondary work at issue in Castle Rock, a 132-page book of trivia about the events and characters depicted in Seinfeld. Despite its specious claims to critique and expose the Seinfeld series, the trivia book served no purpose but "to satiate Seinfeld fans' passion" for the series and simply "repackage[d] Seinfeld to entertain Seinfeld viewers." Castle Rock, 150 F.3d at 142. A statement by the book's creators on the back cover, urging readers to "open this book to satisfy [their] between-episode [Seinfeld] cravings," belied its transformative purpose. Id. By contrast, the Lexicon seeks not to entertain but to aid the reader or student of Harry Potter by providing references about the elements encountered in the series.[19]

The Lexicon's purpose as a reference guide also distinguishes it from the books at issue in Twin Peaks and Paramount Pictures. Those books sought to retell the fictional stories of the Twin Peaks series and the Star Trek series in abridged versions. See Twin Peaks, 996 F.2d at 1372-73, 1375-76 (finding that the book at issue was an "abridgment"

---

[19] Also, unlike the defendants in Castle Rock who used the cachet of Seinfeld on the cover of the trivia book to entice fans, RDR Books has changed the title of the Lexicon to bear no reference to Harry Potter and at Plaintiffs' request added a prominent disclaimer on the book's cover.

because it recounted "precisely the plot details" of television episodes "in the same sequence" as they appeared in the original series); Paramount Pictures, 11 F. Supp. 2d at 335 (finding that the work at issue "simply retells the story of Star Trek in a condensed version"). Because the books in those cases merely recast the originals in abridged versions, they were held to be derivative works. The Lexicon, on the other hand, has a "further purpose or different character," Campbell, 510 U.S. at 579, that alters the original aesthetic of the Harry Potter series from an intricate narrative to an alphabetized catalogue of elements from the Harry Potter world.

Plaintiffs argue that the Lexicon's use of Rowling's works cannot be considered transformative because the Lexicon does not add significant analysis or commentary. In the opinion of Plaintiffs' expert, the Lexicon contributes nothing new other than occasional facetious phrases and facile jokes that are condescending to children (Pl. Ex. 28 (Suppl. Johnson Decl.) ¶ 9; Tr. (Johnson) at 633:8-634:7), sporadic and often wrong etymological references demonstrating "no real linguistic understanding" (Pl. Ex. 28, ¶ 11), and conclusions that would be obvious to any child reading Harry Potter (id. ¶ 7). The Lexicon, however, does not purport to be a work of literary criticism or to constitute a fair use on that basis; and its lack of critical analysis, linguistic understanding, or clever humor is not determinative of whether or not its purpose is transformative.[20] Cf. Bill Graham Archives, 448 F.3d at 610 (concluding that the defendant's use of copyrighted images "is transformative both when accompanied by referencing commentary and when standing alone" because in either case the images are used as "historical artifacts" for the

---

[20] In its original motion papers, Defendant argued that the Lexicon was a work of scholarship. In his testimony at trial, Roger Rapoport maintained this position. Defendant's fair use defense has since changed its angle and no longer characterizes the Lexicon as a scholarly work. Defendant's expert Janet Sorensen admits that the Lexicon book is not a work of scholarship (Tr. (Sorensen) at 538:14-15), and Vander Ark testified that commentary and analysis are not the purpose of the Lexicon (Tr. (Vander Ark) at 283:8-14).

transformative purpose of "enhancing the biographical information" in the allegedly infringing book). Focusing on what the Lexicon fails to add by way of analysis misses the point that the Lexicon's chief contribution is the function it serves.

Nonetheless, despite Plaintiffs' criticisms, the Lexicon occasionally does offer "new information, new aesthetics, new insights and understandings," Castle Rock, 150 F.3d at 141 (internal quotation marks omitted), as to the themes and characters in the Harry Potter works. The Lexicon's discussion of certain characters, while perhaps not rigorous analysis, contain some reflections on the character, observations of his or her nature, and examples of how that nature is exhibited in the story. For example, the Lexicon observes that "Draco [Malfoy] was constantly frustrated by the attention given to Harry," and gives anecdotal examples from the novels to support this conclusion. (See also Pl. Ex. 1, entry for "Longbottom, Neville" (containing observations about the nature of his bravery and leadership); entry for "Lovegood, Luna" (containing observations about her social awkwardness and dignity)). Moreover, in some instances, the Lexicon yields insights about an element of the Harry Potter world simply by encapsulating all the fictional facts related to that element in a single entry. When all the fictional facts related to "Hallowe'en" are collected, for example, the entry reveals that this occasion is "an eventful day in Harry's life; on Hallowe'en 1981 his parents were killed (DH17) and his subsequent years included knocking out a troll (PS10), the opening of the Chamber of Secrets (CS8), Sirius Black's first break-in to Hogwarts (PA8), and Harry's name coming out of the Goblet of Fire (GF16)." Finally, the Lexicon's etymological references, while occasionally inaccurate, offer one possible interpretation of the meaning and derivation of characters' names, even if not the meaning intended by Rowling. Thus, while not its primary purpose, the Lexicon does add some new insight, of whatever value, as to the Harry Potter works.

The transformative character of the Lexicon is diminished, however, because the Lexicon's use of the original Harry Potter works is not consistently transformative. The Lexicon's use lacks transformative character where the Lexicon entries fail to "minimize[] the expressive value" of the original expression. See Bill Graham Archives, 448 F.3d at 611 (finding evidence of transformative use where the defendant "minimized the expressive value of the reproduced images by combining them with a prominent timeline, textual material, and original graphical artwork to create a collage of text and images on each page of the book"). A finding of verbatim copying in excess of what is reasonably necessary diminishes a finding of a transformative use. See Campbell, 510 U.S. at 587 (observing that "whether a substantial portion of the infringing work was copied verbatim from the copyrighted work . . . may reveal a dearth of transformative character" (internal quotation marks omitted)). As discussed more fully in analyzing the "amount and substantiality" factor, the Lexicon copies distinctive original language from the Harry Potter works in excess of its otherwise legitimate purpose of creating a reference guide. Perhaps because Vander Ark is such a Harry Potter enthusiast, the Lexicon often lacks restraint in using Rowling's original expression for its inherent entertainment and aesthetic value. See Elvis Presley Enters., 349 F.3d at 629 (finding that where a film biography of Elvis Presley showed the plaintiffs' copyrighted clips of Elvis's television appearances without much interruption, "[t]he purpose of showing these clips likely goes beyond merely making a reference for a biography, but instead serves the same intrinsic entertainment value that is protected by Plaintiffs' copyrights").

The Lexicon also lacks transformative character where its value as a reference guide lapses. Although the Lexicon is generally useful, it cannot claim consistency in serving its purpose of pointing readers to information in the Harry Potter works. Some of the longest entries contain few or no citations to the Harry Potter works from which the material is taken. (See supra Findings of Fact; Pl. Ex. 28 (Suppl. Johnson Decl.) ¶ 16.) In these instances, the Lexicon's reference purposes are diminished.

While the transformative character of the secondary work is a central inquiry, the commercial or nonprofit nature of the secondary work is an explicit part of the first fair-use factor. 17 U.S.C. 107(1); Blanch, 467 F.3d at 253. Given that even the statutory examples of fair use are generally conducted for profit, courts often "do not make much of this point." Castle Rock, 150 F.3d at 141. The real concern behind the commercial nature inquiry is "the unfairness that arises when a secondary user makes unauthorized use of copyrighted material to capture significant revenues as a direct consequence of copying the original work." Blanch, 467 F.3d at 253. Courts will not find fair use when the secondary use "can fairly be characterized as a form of commercial exploitation," but "are more willing to find a secondary use fair when it produces a value that benefits the broader public interest." Id. In this case, Defendant's use of the copyrighted works is certainly for commercial gain. As the testimony of Rapoport and Vander Ark make clear, one of the Lexicon's greatest selling points is being the first companion guide to the Harry Potter series that will cover all seven novels. Seeking to capitalize on a market niche does not necessarily make Defendant's use non-transformative, but to the extent that Defendant seeks to "profit at least in part from the inherent entertainment value" of the original works, the commercial nature of the use weighs against a finding of fair use.

Elvis Presley Enters., 349 F.3d at 628. To the extent that Defendant seeks to provide a useful reference guide to the Harry Potter novels that benefits the public, the use is fair, and its commercial nature only weighs slightly against a finding of fair use.

Finally, in evaluating the purpose and character of a secondary use of a copyrighted work, courts will consider the "subfactor" of whether the defendant acted in good or bad faith. NXIVM Corp. v. Ross Inst., 364 F.3d 471, 478 (2d Cir. 2004); see also Harper & Row, 471 U.S. at 562-63. Plaintiffs point to several facts in the record to support their argument that Defendant acted with willfulness and bad faith. The Court is not persuaded, however, that the acts of RDR Books, which do not amount to more than intentional delays in responding to Plaintiffs' communications from counsel, constitute acts of bad faith.[21] Based on the reasonable belief that its use of the Harry Potter works constituted fair use, Defendant was entitled to proceed with marketing the Lexicon domestically and abroad and preparing it for publication before competitors released similar books. Vander Ark's use of unauthorized electronic copies of Rowling's works, obtained by improperly scanning each of those works, in preparing the Lexicon manuscript is insufficient proof for the Court to make a finding of bad faith, particularly because Vander Ark did not obtain any material that was not already available to the public. Compare NXIVM Corp., 364 F.3d at 478 (weighing this factor slightly in favor of plaintiffs because defendants knew they had obtained unauthorized access to the copyrighted manuscript, which was unpublished in the sense it was not available to the general public). In any event, as the Second Circuit has concluded, "a finding of bad faith is not to be weighed very heavily within the first fair use factor and cannot be made

---

[21] Nor does the Court find Defendant's allegations of Plaintiffs' copyright misuse and unclean hands to amount to more than aggressive protective actions permitted by copyright law. Defendant apparently agreed, as it abandoned these defenses by the end of trial.

central to fair use analysis." Id. at 479 n.2. This subfactor weighs only slightly in favor of Plaintiffs, as the Court finds that Defendant reasonably believed its use was ultimately fair.

### B. Amount and Substantiality of the Use

Plaintiffs contend that the Lexicon's actual use of Plaintiffs' original works far surpasses any purpose as a reference source. They argue, in other words, that the Lexicon takes too much original expression for the use to be fair use. Here, the transformative purpose of Defendant's use and the third statutory factor of fair use—the amount and substantiality of the use—must be "explored, and the results weighed together." Campbell, 510 U.S. at 577-78. The question is whether the amount and value of Plaintiffs' original expression used are reasonable in relation to the Lexicon's transformative purpose of creating a useful and complete A-to-Z reference guide to the Harry Potter world. See Campbell, 510 U.S. at 586 (stating that the third factor asks whether the amount and substantiality of the portion used in relation to the copyrighted work as a whole "are reasonable in relation to the purpose of the copying"); Blanch, 467 F.2d at 257 ("The question is whether 'the quantity and value of the materials used,' are reasonable in relation to the purpose of the copying."); see also Chicago Bd. of Educ. v. Substance, Inc., 354 F.3d 624, 629 (7th Cir. 2003) (stating that "the fair use copier must copy no more than is reasonably necessary . . . to enable him to pursue an aim that the law recognizes as proper"). This inquiry requires the Court to examine not only "the quantity of the materials used, but their quality and importance, too." Campbell, 510 U.S. at 587; Nihon Keizai Shimbun, 166 F.3d at 73. Blanch, 467 F.2d at 257 ("The question is whether 'the quantity and value of the materials used,' are reasonable in relation to the [transformative] purpose of the copying.").

In undertaking this inquiry, the Court bears in mind that "room must be allowed for judgment, and judges must not police criticism," or other transformative uses, "with a heavy hand." Chicago Bd. of Educ., 354 F.3d at 629. The Court is hesitant to substitute its own judgment for that of an author in determining how much copying of original material is "reasonably necessary" to create a useful and complete reference work. Nonetheless, the fair use test calls for a court determination on this issue.

To fulfill its purpose as a reference guide to the Harry Potter works, it is reasonably necessary for the Lexicon to make considerable use of the original works. As Vander Ark testified, for a reference work to be valuable and useful, it must be as complete as possible. (Tr. (Vander Ark) at 281:20-21, 369:23-25.) Similarly, in Ty, Inc. v. Publications International Ltd., the Seventh Circuit recognized that for a collectors' guide to have enough value "to compete in the marketplace, [it] has to be comprehensive." 292 F.3d at 521. At trial, Plaintiffs questioned Vander Ark and Defendants' expert about whether it was possible to create a reference book that took less of Rowling's work and gave shorter descriptions. (Id. (Vander Ark) at 281:10-282:6; id. (Sorensen) at 543:23-546:316-20.) While it is *possible* to describe "Albus Dumbledore"[22] or "Bertie Bott's Every Flavor Beans,"[23] for example, in a few phrases, such a short entry would not fulfill the Lexicon's purpose of serving as a useful reference

---

[22] To demonstrate that "Albus Dumbledore" could be described without using Rowling's words or details from the novels, Plaintiffs use the testimony of Defendant's expert, identifying Dumbledore as "the master of Hogwarts in Harry's time there and for decades before that. He's one of the main characters. He's sort of very wise, almost a kind of father figure to Harry. He is the leader of the sort of good force in the novel." (Tr. (Sorensen) at 514:13-18.)

[23] Plaintiffs suggest that the Lexicon could have described "Bertie Bott's Every Flavor Beans" as follows: "A favorite candy in the wizarding world, similar to jellybeans but with unexpected and sometimes disgusting flavors." (Pl. Post-trial Br. at 42.)

guide that provides the reader or student with as complete a picture as possible of the entry's subject.

Weighing most heavily against Defendant on the third factor is the Lexicon's verbatim copying and close paraphrasing of language from the Harry Potter works. In many instances, the copied language is a colorful literary device or distinctive description, as in the Lexicon entries for "Clankers," "Marchbanks, Madam Griselda," "Brain room," and "Dementors." See supra Findings of Fact. This type of langauge is of great quality and importance; these phrases are, as Rowling testified, the "plums in [her] cake." (Tr. (Rowling) at 647:3-6). The Lexicon's verbatim copying of such highly aesthetic expression raises a significant question as to whether it was reasonably necessary for the purpose of creating a useful and complete reference guide. While the exact quantity of verbatim copying and paraphrasing in the Lexicon is difficult to assess, the instances identified by Plaintiffs amount to a substantial enough taking to tip the third factor against a finding of fair use in view of the expressive value of the language. See Harper & Row, 471 U.S. at 564-66 (finding that defendant's verbatim copying, constituting "an insubstantial portion" of the copyrighted work and only 13% of the infringing magazine article, was a substantial appropriation in view of the expressive value of the excerpts and their key role in the infringing work); Salinger v. Random House, Inc., 811 F.2d 90, 99 (2d Cir. 1987) (finding that defendant's biography, in which plaintiff identified 59 instances of verbatim quoting or close paraphrasing (constituting just 40% of defendant's 192-page book), to be so quantitatively significant a taking so as to tip the third factor in favor of plaintiff); Craft v. Kobler, 667 F. Supp. 120, 128-29 (S.D.N.Y. 1987) (concluding that defendant's takings, which constituted approximately

3% of the infringing biography and "the liveliest and most entertaining part" of it, were "far too numerous and with too little instructional justification to support the conclusion of fair use").

Defendant argues that it is impossible to describe an imaginary object that exists only in a fictional world without using some of the language that invented it. Certainly, the Lexicon must be permitted to refer to an object by its invented name and describe some of its invented attributes to fulfill its purpose as a reference work; but again, the use must be reasonable in light of that purpose. The imaginary objects "clankers," for example, can be successfully described without using the original literary device ("like miniature hammers on anvils") and the original turn of phrase ("a number of small metal instruments that when shaken made a loud, ringing noise") that brought them into existence. As the Second Circuit noted in Salinger v. Random House, Inc., a copier is not entitled to copy the vividness of an author's description for the sake of accurately reporting expressive content. 811 F.2d at 96-97. Moreover, in some entries, the Lexicon copies original expression verbatim even when describing objects that are ordinary and exist in the real world. For example, the Lexicon entry for "Mirror of Erised" replicates Rowling's original language from Harry Potter and the Sorcerer's Stone to describe a mirror: "A magnificent mirror, as high as a classroom ceiling, with an ornate gold frame, standing on two clawed feet." (See supra Findings of Fact.) Verbatim copying of this nature demonstrates Vander Ark's lack of restraint due to an enthusiastic admiration of Rowling's artistic expression, or perhaps haste and laziness as Rowling suggested (Tr. (Rowling) at 62:18-20), in composing the Lexicon entries.

Determining how much copying of fictional facts and plot elements from the Harry Potter series is reasonably necessary to create a useful and complete reference guide presents a difficult task. As Vander Ark testified, "[a] reference work of th[is] kind has to have value based on how much information it gives, and so it is difficult sometimes to figure out the balance. And we tried to do the best we could to find a balance between" creating shorter descriptions that take less copyrighted material and creating a valuable entry that is as complete as possible. (Tr. (Vander Ark) at 281:20-23.) As to the Harry Potter series, the Lexicon often does demonstrate a significant condensation of narrated events in the novels to bare fictional facts. For example, the entry for "Boggart" encapsulates Professor Lupin's Defense Against the Dark Arts lesson on how to use the Riddikulus spell to defeat a boggart, spanning seven pages of lively narration and dialogue (see Pl. Ex. 6 at 133-39), in one colorless phrase: "Lupin taught his third year Defence Against the Dark Arts class to fight this with the Riddikulus spell (PA7)." (Compare also Pl. Ex. 6 at 236-42, with Pl. Ex. 1, entry for "Boggart" (stating that Lupin "used a boggart as a substitute for a Dementor in tutoring Harry (PA12)").) Other times, however, the Lexicon disturbs the balance and takes more than is reasonably necessary to create a reference guide. In these instances, the Lexicon appears to retell parts of the storyline rather than report fictional facts and where to find them. For example, the Lexicon entry for "Trelawney, Sibyll Patricia" not only copies exactly the Divination professor's prophecies about the fates of Voldemort, Harry Potter, and Peter Pettigrew, it then tells how the prophecies are fulfilled, including events that do not involve Trelawney. (Compare also Pl. Ex. 10 at 714-720, with Pl. Ex. 1, entry for "Deathly Hallows, The," ¶ 5 (retelling the story that Dumbledore tells Harry about his own quest for the Hallows with Grindelwald in Chapter 35 of the seventh novel).) While it is difficult to draw the line at each entry that takes more than is reasonably necessary from the Harry Potter series to serve its purposes, there are a number of places where the Lexicon engages in the same sort of extensive borrowing that might be expected of a copyright owner,[24] not a third party author.

The Lexicon's use of copyrighted expression from Rowling's two companion books presents an easier determination. The Lexicon takes wholesale from these short books. See supra Findings of Fact. Depending on the purpose, using a substantial portion of a work, or even the whole thing, may be permissible. See, e.g., Perfect 10, 518 F.3d at 1167-68; Bill Graham Archives, 448 F.3d at 613; Nunez v. Caribbean v. Int'l News Corp., 235 F.3d 18, 24 (1st Cir. 2000). In this case, however, the Lexicon's purpose is only slightly transformative of the companion books' original purpose. As a result, the amount and substantiality of the portion copied from the companion books weighs more heavily against a finding of fair use.

### C. Nature of the Copyrighted Work

The second statutory fair use factor, the nature of the copyrighted work, recognizes that "some works are closer to the core of intended copyright protection than others." Campbell, 510 U.S. at 586. It is well settled that creative and fictional works are generally more deserving of protection than factual works. Stewart v. Abend, DBA Authors Research Co., 495 U.S. 207, 237 (1990) ("In general, fair use is more likely to be found in factual works than in fictional works."); Harper & Row, 471 U.S. at 563 ("The law generally recognizes a greater need to disseminate factual works than works of

---

[24] In fact, the Lexicon borrows from the Harry Potter works with approximately the same liberty that the Companion to Narnia (Pl. Ex. 62), written by third-party author Paul F. Ford and published by copyright holder HarperCollins, borrows from C.S. Lewis's The Chronicles of Narnia.

fiction or fantasy."); Castle Rock, 150 F.3d at 143-144 (finding that the second factor favored plaintiff given the fictional nature of the copyrighted work); Twin Peaks, 996 F.2d at 1376 (stating that the second factor "must favor a creative and fictional work, no matter how successful"); Ty, Inc. v. Publ'ns Int'l, Ltd., 333 F. Supp. 2d 705, 713 (N.D. Ill. 2004) (recognizing that "creative works are deemed more deserving of protection than works that are more of diligence than of originality or inventiveness." (internal quotation marks omitted)). In creating the Harry Potter novels and the companion books, Rowling has given life to a wholly original universe of people, creatures, places, and things. (Tr. (Sorensen) at 504:7-15). Such highly imaginative and creative fictional works are close to the core of copyright protection, particularly where the character of the secondary work is not entirely transformative. See Castle Rock, 150 F.3d at 144; Twin Peaks, 996 F.2d at 1376; Paramount, 11 F. Supp. 2d at 336. As a result, the second factor favors Plaintiffs.

**D. Market Harm**

The fourth statutory factor considers "the effect of the use upon the potential market for or value of the copyrighted work." 17 U.S.C. § 107(4). Courts must consider harm to "not only the primary market for the copyrighted work, but the current and potential market for derivative works" as well. Twin Peaks, 996 F.2d at 1377 (finding that fourth factor favored plaintiff where book about television series "may interfere with the primary market for the copyrighted works and almost certainly interferes with legitimate markets for derivative works"); see also Harper & Row, 471 U.S. at 568. Potential derivative uses "include[] only those that creators of original works would in general develop or license others to develop." Campbell, 510 U.S. at 592. The fourth factor will favor the copyright holder "if she can show a 'traditional, reasonable, or likely to be developed' market for licensing her work." Ringgold, 126 F.3d at 81. In addition to evaluating the particular actions of the alleged infringer, the fourth factor examines "whether unrestricted and widespread conduct of the sort engaged in by the defendant . . . would result in a substantially adverse impact on the potential market for the original." Campbell, 510 U.S. at 590 (omission in original) (internal quotation marks and citations omitted).

Plaintiffs presented expert testimony that the Lexicon would compete directly with, and impair the sales of, Rowling's planned encyclopedia by being first to market. (Tr. (Murphy) at 413:2-416:6, 417:21-418:9.) Defendant rebutted this evidence with its own expert who testified that publication of the Lexicon is "extremely unlikely" to affect the sales of any encyclopedia that Rowling might one day publish. (Id. (Harris) at 442:9-16.) This testimony does not bear on the determination of the fourth factor, however, because a reference guide to the Harry Potter works is not a derivative work; competing with Rowling's planned encyclopedia is therefore permissible. Notwithstanding Rowling's public statements of her intention to publish her own encyclopedia, the market for reference guides to the Harry Potter works is not exclusively hers to exploit or license, no matter the commercial success attributable to the popularity of the original works. See Twin Peaks, 996 F.2d at 1377 ("The author of 'Twin Peaks' cannot preserve for itself the entire field of publishable works that wish to cash in on the 'Twin Peaks' phenomenon"). The market for reference guides does not become derivative simply because the copyright holder seeks to produce or license one. Ty, Inc., 292 F.3d at 521; see also Castle Rock, 150 F.3d at 145 n.11 ("[B]y developing or licensing a market for parody, news reporting, educational or other transformative uses of its own creative work, a copyrighted owner plainly cannot prevent others from entering those fair use markets"); Twin Peaks, 996 F.2d at 1377.

Furthermore, there is no plausible basis to conclude that publication of the Lexicon would impair sales of the Harry Potter novels. Plaintiffs' expert Suzanne Murphy, vice president and publisher of trade publishing and marketing at Scholastic, testified that in her opinion a child who read the Lexicon would be discouraged from reading the Harry Potter series because the Lexicon discloses key plot points and does not contain "spoiler alerts." (Tr. (Murphy) at 409:12-411:7.) Children may be an elusive market for book publishers, but it is hard to believe that a child, having read the Lexicon, would lose interest in reading (and thus his or her parents' interest in purchasing) the Harry Potter series. Because the Lexicon uses the Harry Potter series for a transformative purpose (though inconsistently), reading the Lexicon cannot serve as a substitute for reading the original novels; they are enjoyed for different purposes. The Lexicon is thus unlikely to serve as a market substitute for the Harry Potter series and cause market harm. Campbell, 510 U.S. at 591 (stating that when "the second use is transformative, market substitution is at least less certain and market harm may not be so readily inferred"); see also Castle Rock, 150 F.3d at 145; Bill Graham Archives, 448 F.3d at 614-15. It seems unlikely that a publisher like HarperCollins would produce the Companion to Narnia (Pl. Ex. 62), which reveals storylines, plot twists, and the ultimate fates of the characters in C.S. Lewis's original works, if it expected the publication would reduce sales and enthusiasm for the original works. Accordingly, the Lexicon does not present any potential harm to the markets for the original Harry Potter works. See Bill Graham Archives, 448 F.3d at 614; Castle Rock, 150 F.3d at 145.

On the other hand, publication of the Lexicon could harm sales of Rowling's two companion books. Unless they sought to enjoy the companion books for their entertainment value alone, consumers who purchased the Lexicon would have scant incentive to purchase either of Rowling's companion books, as the information contained in these short works has been incorporated into the Lexicon almost wholesale. (Tr. (Murphy) at 419:10-19; id. (Rowling) at 104:2-11.) Because the Lexicon's use of the companion books is only marginally transformative, the Lexicon is likely to supplant the market for the companion books. See Campbell, 510 U.S. at 591 (stating that "when a commercial use amounts to mere duplication of the entirety of an original, it clearly 'supersede[s] the objects' of the original and serves as a market replacement for it, making it likely that cognizable harm to the original will occur" (citation omitted)). At trial, Vander Ark himself recognized that although "[t]here's no way that someone's going to take an encyclopedia of [the Harry Potter novels] and think of it as a replacement" (Tr. (Vander Ark) at 287:14-16), using the companion books without "replac[ing] Ms. Rowling's encyclopedia content" presents "quite a challenge" (id. at 287:22-25). In view of the market harm to Rowling's companion books, the fourth factor tips in favor of Plaintiffs.

Additionally, the fourth factor favors Plaintiffs if publication of the Lexicon would impair the market for derivative works that Rowling is entitled or likely to license. Ringgold, 126 F.3d at 81. Although there is no supporting testimony, one potential derivative market that would reasonably be developed or licensed by Plaintiffs is use of the songs and poems in the Harry Potter novels. Because Plaintiffs would reasonably license the musical production or print publication of those songs and poems, Defendant unfairly harms this derivative market by reproducing verbatim the songs and poems without a license.

* * *

The fair-use factors, weighed together in light of the purposes of copyright law, fail to support the defense of fair use in this case. The first factor does not completely weigh in favor of Defendant because although the Lexicon has a transformative purpose, its actual use of the copyrighted works is not consistently transformative. Without drawing a line at the amount of copyrighted material that is reasonably necessary to create an A-to-Z reference guide, many portions of the Lexicon take more of the copyrighted works than is reasonably necessary in relation to the Lexicon's purpose. Thus, in balancing the first and third factors, the balance is tipped against a finding of fair use. The creative nature of the copyrighted works and the harm to the market for Rowling's companion books weigh in favor of Plaintiffs. In striking the balance between the property rights of original authors and the freedom of expression of secondary authors, reference guides to works of literature should generally be encouraged by copyright law as they provide a benefit readers and students; but to borrow from Rowling's overstated views, they should not be permitted to "plunder" the works of original authors (Tr. (Rowling) at 62:25-63:3), "without paying the customary price" Harper & Row, 471 U.S. at 562, lest original authors lose incentive to create new works that will also benefit the public interest (see Tr. (Rowling) at 93:20-94:13).

## III. Injunctive and Statutory Relief

The Copyright Act provides that courts "may" grant injunctive relief "on such terms as it may deem reasonable to prevent or restrain infringement of a copyright." 17 U.S.C. § 502(a). In eBay Inc. v. MercExchange, L.L.C., the Supreme Court made clear that an injunction does not automatically follow a determination that a copyright has been infringed. 547 U.S. 388, 392-93 (2006). A copyright plaintiff seeking a permanent injunction still must satisfy the traditional four-factor test before the district court may use its equitable discretion to grant such relief. The plaintiff must demonstrate: (1) that it will suffer an irreparable injury; (2) that remedies available at law, such as monetary damages, are inadequate to compensate for that injury; (3) that, considering the balance of hardships between the plaintiff and defendant, a remedy in equity is warranted; and (4) that the public interest would not be disserved by a permanent injunction. See Weinberger v. Romero-Barcelo, 456 U.S. 305, 311-13 (1982); Amoco Production Co. v. Gambell, 480 U.S. 531, 542 (1987).

### A. Irreparable Injury

Under the law of this Circuit, "generally when a copyright plaintiff makes out a prima facie showing of infringement, irreparable harm may be presumed." ABKCO Music, Inc. v. Stellar Records, Inc., 96 F.3d 60, 66 (2d Cir. 1996). Because Plaintiffs have demonstrated a case of copyright infringement, and because Defendant has failed to establish its affirmative defense to copyright infringement, irreparable injury may be presumed in this case. In view of eBay, which applied the traditional four-part test for injunctive relief in the context of a patent claim, there is some question of whether the presumption of irreparable harm still applies. District courts, however, have continued to apply the presumption post-eBay. See, e.g., Warner Bros. Entm't Inc. v. Carsagno, No. 06 Civ. 2676, 2007 WL 1655666, *6 (E.D.N.Y. June 4, 2007) (finding irreparable harm where plaintiff had demonstrated that without an injunction, its copyrighted work would be subject to continued copyright infringement); UMG Recordings, Inc. v. Blake, No. 06 Civ. 00120, 2007 WL 1853956, *3 (E.D.N.C. June 26, 2007) (stating that irreparable injury is presumed when plaintiff succeeds on the merits).

Regardless, even if irreparable injury is not presumed, Plaintiffs have presented sufficient evidence that such injury would result from Defendant's infringement in the absence of relief. First, Plaintiffs have established that publication of the Lexicon will cause irreparable injury to Rowling as a writer. Rowling testified that if the Lexicon is published, it would destroy her "will or heart to continue with [writing her own] encyclopedia." (Tr. (Rowling) at 54:9-12.) She further testified that if the Lexicon is published—giving "carte blanche to . . . anyone who wants to make a quick bit of money" by drawing freely from her works and opening the doors to "a surfeit of substandard so-called lexicons and guides"—she would have much less incentive to write her own book. (Tr. (Rowling) at 54:4-12.) By deterring Rowling from writing her planned encyclopedia, publication of the Lexicon would also result in harm to the charitable organizations that would receive the royalties from the sale of the book and the reading public who would be unable to enjoy such a book. (Tr. (Rowling) at 55:1-5.)

More concretely, publication of the Lexicon would cause irreparable harm to the sales of Rowling's companion books, all the elements of which are replicated in the Lexicon for a similar purpose. Readers would have no reason to purchase the companion books since the Lexicon supersedes their value. (Tr. (Rowling) at 101:25-102:12.)

Additionally, because the Lexicon engages in considerable verbatim copying of the Harry Potter works, publication of the Lexicon would diminish Rowling's copyright in her own language. Based on evidence of Vander Ark's vigorous claim to his rights in the Lexicon website (Tr. (Rowling) at 100:18-101:7; id. (Vander Ark) at 312:6-313:13), publication of the Lexicon may result in conflicting assertions of copyright over the same material by Rowling on one hand and Vander Ark or RDR Books on the other. (See Tr. (Rowling) 96:10-11, 14-23 (noting her concern that if she published her own encyclopedia, RDR Books would sue her for copyright infringement, claiming that her "paraphrase ran a little too close to [Vander Ark's] paraphrasing").)

### B. Inadequate Remedies at Law

If an injunction is not issued, Defendant is likely to continue infringing Plaintiffs' copyright in the future. RDR Books has actively marketed the Lexicon domestically and abroad (see supra Findings of Fact) and might gain considerable commercial success as the first Harry Potter reference guide to hit the market after Rowling's completion of the series. (Tr. (Vander Ark) at 255:7-14, 361:9-15; id. (Murphy) at 413:24-414:24; see Pl. Ex. 14N.) In view of the irreparable harm that would flow from Defendant's continuing infringement, including lost sales of Rowling's companion books and the injury to Rowling as a writer, Plaintiffs have shown that money damages alone are an insufficient remedy. See Lauratex Textile Corp. v. Allton Knitting Mills Inc., 519 F. Supp. 730, 732 (S.D.N.Y. 1981) (finding that money damages would not suffice where there was a strong probability that the defendant would continue to infringe plaintiff's copyright).

### C. Balance of Hardships

While Plaintiffs have identified their hardships if an injunction were not granted, Defendant identifies no hardship it would suffer if publication of the Lexicon were enjoined. The only possible harm to Defendant is the loss of the chance to sell an infringing book, but the law does not protect this type of hardship. See My-T Fine Corp. v. Samuels, 69 F.2d 76, 78 (2d Cir. 1934) (Hand, J.); see also Concrete Mach. Co. v. Classic Lawn Ornaments, 843 F.2d 600, 612 (1st Cir. 1988); Apple Computer Inc. v. Franklin Computer Corp., 714 F.2d 1240, 1255 (3d Cir. 1983). Thus, the balance of the hardships weighs in favor of Plaintiffs.

### D. Public Interest

Issuing an injunction in this case both benefits and harms the public interest. While the Lexicon, in its current state, is not a fair use of the Harry Potter works, reference works that share the Lexicon's purpose of aiding readers of literature generally should be encouraged rather than stifled. As the Supreme Court suggested in Campbell, "[b]ecause the fair use enquiry often requires close questions of judgment as to the extent of permissible borrowing" in cases involving transformative uses, granting an injunction does not always serve the goals of copyright law, when the secondary use, though edifying in some way, has been found to surpass the bounds of fair use. Campbell, 510 U.S. at 578 n.10. On the other hand, to serve the public interest, copyright law must "prevent[] the misappropriation of the skills, creative energies, and resources which are invested in the protected work." Apple Computer, 714 F.2d at 1255. Ultimately, because the Lexicon appropriates too much of Rowling's creative work for its purposes as a reference guide, a permanent injunction must issue to prevent the possible proliferation of works that do the same[25] and thus deplete the incentive for original authors to create new works.

In addition to injunctive relief, Plaintiffs seek statutory damages in this case. Under the Copyright Act, a plaintiff may elect to recover an award of statutory damages for each infringed work "in a sum of not less than $750 or more than $30,000 as the court considers just." 17 U.S.C. § 504. In awarding statutory damages, courts have broad discretion to set the amount of the award within the statutory limits. Fitzgerald Publ'g Co. v. Baylor Publ'g Co., 807 F.2d 1110, 1116-17 (2d Cir. 1986). Since the Lexicon has not been published and thus Plaintiffs have suffered no harm beyond the fact of infringement, the Court awards Plaintiffs the minimum award under the statute for each work with respect to which Plaintiffs have established infringement. Plaintiffs are entitled to statutory damages of $750.00 for each of the seven Harry Potter novels and each of the two companion books, for a total of $6,750.00.

**CONCLUSION**

For the foregoing reasons, Plaintiffs have established copyright infringement of the Harry Potter series, Fantastic Beasts & Where to Find Them, and Quidditch Through the Ages by J.K. Rowling. Defendant has failed to establish its affirmative defense of

---

[25] See Tr. (Murphy) at 419:24-2 (stating her opinion that publication of the Lexicon would open the doors to widespread creation of works that copy too much from the Harry Potter works).

fair use. Defendant's publication of the Lexicon (Doc. No. 22) is hereby permanently enjoined, and Plaintiffs are awarded statutory damages of $6,750.00.

    IT IS SO ORDERED.

Dated: New York, New York
        September 8, 2008

                                                          Robert P. Patterson, Jr.
                                                                   U.S.D.J.

**Copies of this Order sent to:**

*Attorneys for Plaintiffs*
O'Melveny & Myers LLP
Attn: Dale Margaret Cendali
7 Times Square
New York, NY 10036
Tel: 212-326-2000
Fax: 212-326-2061

*Attorney for Defendant*
David S. Hammer
110 Green St., Suite 1101
New York, NY 10012
Tel: 212-941-8118